The Treasure of

Maurice Maeterlinck

(Translator: Alfred Sutro)

Alpha Editions

This edition published in 2024

ISBN : 9789361475160

Design and Setting By
Alpha Editions
www.alphaedis.com
Email - info@alphaedis.com

As per information held with us this book is in Public Domain.
This book is a reproduction of an important historical work. Alpha Editions uses the best technology to reproduce historical work in the same manner it was first published to preserve its original nature. Any marks or number seen are left intentionally to preserve its true form.

Contents

INTRODUCTION .... - 1 -
SILENCE .... - 5 -
THE AWAKENING OF THE SOUL .... - 11 -
THE PRE-DESTINED .... - 17 -
MYSTIC MORALITY .... - 21 -
ON WOMEN .... - 25 -
THE TRAGICAL IN DAILY LIFE .... - 31 -
THE STAR .... - 38 -
THE INVISIBLE GOODNESS .... - 45 -
THE DEEPER LIFE .... - 51 -
THE INNER BEAUTY .... - 59 -

INTRODUCTION

WITH M. Maeterlinck as a dramatist the world is pretty well acquainted. This little volume presents him in the new character of a philosopher and an æsthetician. And it is in some sort an 'apology' for his theatre, the one being to the other as theory to practice. Reversing the course prescribed by Mr. Squeers for his pupils, M. Maeterlinck, having cleaned w-i-n-d-e-r, winder, now goes and spells it. He began by visualising and synthetising his ideas of life; here you shall find him trying to analyse these ideas and consumed with anxiety to tell us the truth that is in him. It is not a truth for all markets; he is at no pains to conceal that. He appeals, as every mystic must, to the elect; M. Anatole France would say, to the *âmes bien nées*. If we are not sealed of the tribe of Plotinus, he warns us to go elsewhere. 'If, plunging thine eyes into thyself—it is this same Plotinus that he is quoting—'thou dost not feel the charm of beauty, it is in vain that, thy disposition being such, thou shouldst seek the charm of beauty; for thou wouldst seek it only with that which is ugly and impure. Therefore it is that the discourse we hold here is not addressed to all men.' If we are to follow him in his expedition to a philosophic Ultima Thule, we must have the mind for that adventure. 'We are here,' as he tells us elsewhere of the 'stiff' but, it seems, 'admirable' Ruysbroeck, 'all of a sudden on the borderland of human thought and far across the Arctic circle of the spirit. There is no ordinary cold, no ordinary dark there, and yet you shall find there naught but flames and light. But to those who arrive without having trained their minds to these new perceptions, the light and the flames are as dark and as cold as though they were painted.' This means that the intelligence, the reason, will not suffice of themselves; we must have faith. There are passages in the book which may provoke a sniff from Mr. Worldly Wiseman; but we must beware of the Voltairean spirit, or this will be a closed book to us. 'We live by admiration, hope, and love,' said Wordsworth. And we understand by them, M. Maeterlinck would add. I fear we are not all of us found worthy of the mystical frame of mind. But it is a psychological fact, like another; and if we can only examine it from the outside, we can at least bring patience and placidity to the task. The point is: has M. Maeterlinck anything to say? It will be found, I think, that he has.

All men, the world has long been assured, are born Aristotelians or Platonists. There cannot be a doubt about M. Maeterlinck's philosophic birthright. He may say, as Paul Verlaine sang:

Moi, j'allais rêvant du divin Platon,
Sous l'œil clignotant des bleus becs de gaz.

More strictly, he is a Neo-Platonist. His remark about the Admirable Ruysbroeck's idea is equally true of his own. 'I fancy that all those who have not lived in the intimacy of Plato and of the Neo-Platonists of Alexandria, will not go far with this reading.' He quotes Plotinus, 'the great Plotinus, who, of all the intellects known to me, draws the nearest to the divine.' He cites Porphyry and the Gnostics and Swedenborg. These are not exactly popular authors of the moment. But M. Maeterlinck, it is plain, has devoured them; his is not what Pope called 'index-learning.' Plotinus (205-270 A.D.) stood between two worlds, the old and the new; and he made the best of both. He enlarged the boundaries of art by discerning in the idea of beauty an inward and spiritual grace not to be found in the 'Platonic idea.' That, too, is what M. Maeterlinck is striving for: a larger idea of beauty, and a better apprehension of its inward and spiritual grace.

His cardinal doctrine will, I conjecture, prove to be something like this. What should be of most account for us all is not external fact, but the supra-sensuous world. 'What we know is not interesting'; the really interesting things are those which we can only divine—the veiled life of the soul, the crepuscular region of subconsciousness, our 'borderland' feelings, all that lies in the strange 'neutral zone' between the frontiers of consciousness and unconsciousness. The mystery of life is what makes life worth living. '"Twas a little being of mystery, like every one else,' says the old King Arkel of the dead Mélisande. We are such stuff as dreams are made of, might be the 'refrain' of all M. Maeterlinck's plays, and of most of these essays. He is penetrated by the feeling of the mystery in all human creatures, whose every act is regulated by far-off influences and obscurely rooted in things unexplained. Mystery is within us and around us. Of reality we can only get now and then the merest glimpse. Our senses are too gross. Between the invisible world and our own there is doubtless an intimate concordance; but it escapes us. We grope among shadows towards the unknown. Even the new conquests of what we vainly suppose to be 'exact' thought only deepen the mystery of life. There is, for example, the Schopenhauerian theory of love. We had fancied we could at least choose our loves in freedom: but 'we are told that a thousand centuries divide us from ourselves when we choose the woman we love, and that the first kiss of the betrothed is but the seal which thousands of hands, craving for birth, have impressed upon the lips of the mother they desire.' And so with the 'heredity' of the men of science. 'We know that the dead do not die. We know that it is not in our churches they are to be found, but in the houses, the habits of us all.' What was there in the old notion of Destiny so mysterious as this double thraldom of ours—thraldom to the dead and to the unborn? Conclusion: mysticism is your only wear. In the mystics alone is certitude. 'If it be true, as has been said, that every man is a Shakespeare in his dreams, we have to ask ourselves whether every man, in his waking life, is not an inarticulate mystic, a thousandfold more transcendental than those circumscribed by speech.' In silence is our only chance of knowing one another. And 'mystic truths have over ordinary truths a strange privilege; they can neither age nor die.' From all this you see M. Maeterlinck's train of thought. He would fix our minds upon the obscure, pre-conscious, what M. Faguet calls the *incunabulary* life of the soul. He finds no epithets too fine for this: the higher life, the transcendental life, the divine life, the absolute life.

Whatever we may think of these ideas in themselves, there is no doubt that the man who expresses them sounds a new and individual note. They show a reaction against the whole effort of modern literature, which has been nothing if not positive, quasi-scientific, ever on the prowl for 'documents.' And if for no other reason than that, this book, I submit, would have peculiar significance and value.

But there is at least one other reason. M. Maeterlinck puts forward a plea, and a plea not lightly to be dismissed, for a new æsthetic of the drama. The mystery which he finds everywhere around us and within us he would bring into the theatre. If there is one position which the whole world supposed itself to have definitively taken up, it is the position that the theatre lives by action and to offer us an exhibition of the will. Therein, for instance, M. Ferdinand Brunetière finds the *differentia* of drama; it is the struggle of a will, conscious of itself, against obstacles. Traversing this position M. Maeterlinck boldly asks whether a 'static' theatre is impossible, a theatre of mood not of movement, a theatre where nothing material happens and where everything immaterial is felt. Even as it is, the real beauty and purport of a tragedy is not seldom to be found in that part of its dialogue which is superficially 'useless.' 'Certain it is that in the ordinary drama the indispensable dialogue by no means corresponds to reality.... One may even affirm that the poem draws the nearer to beauty and loftier truth in the measure that it eliminates words that merely explain the action and replaces them by others that reveal not the so-called "soul-state," but I know not what intangible and unceasing striving of the soul towards its beauty and its truth.' The frivolous will be reminded here, perhaps, of the old stage direction for the miser: 'Leans against a wall and grows generous.' Others who remember their Xenophon will bethink them of a certain discussion which Socrates had with Parrhasius on the question, 'Can the unseen be imitated?' (*Soc. Memorabilia*, iii. 10). It may be that M. Maeterlinck's 'static' theatre is an unrealisable dream; but it is a seductive one, by contrast with the reality. Do not all of us who are condemned to spend much of our time in the playhouse occasionally share M. Maeterlinck's feeling of repugnance? 'When I go to the theatre, I feel as though I were spending a few hours in the midst of my ancestors, who looked upon life as something that was primitive, arid, and brutal; but this conception of theirs scarcely even lingers in my memory, and surely it is not one that I can any longer share.... I had hoped to be shown some act of life traced back to its source and to its mystery by connecting links that my daily occupations afford me neither power nor occasion to study. I had gone thither hoping that the beauty, the grandeur, and the earnestness of my humble day-by-day existence would for one instant be revealed to me ... whereas, almost invariably, all that I beheld was but a man who would tell me at wearisome length why he was jealous, why he poisoned, or why he killed.' And so he would have the drama make an effort to show us 'how truly wonderful is the mere fact of living'; he would have it tackle 'presentiments, the strange impression produced by a chance meeting or a look, a decision that the unknown side of human reason had governed, an intervention or a force inexplicable and yet understood, the secret laws of sympathy and antipathy, elective and instinctive affinities, the overwhelming influence of things unsaid.'

How is it all to come about? When we ask this question we find ourselves in the position of the lady who had been discussing the subject of a future state with Dr. Johnson. 'She seemed desirous of knowing more,' says Boswell, 'but he left the question in obscurity.' It is there that M. Maeterlinck, like a true mystic, is content to leave most of his questions. 'The time has not yet come,' he says with an engaging candour, 'when we can speak lucidly of these things.' One thinks of Sir Thomas Browne's quaint fancy. 'A dialogue between two infants in the womb concerning the state of this world might handsomely illustrate our ignorance of the next, whereof methinks we yet discourse in Plato's den, and are but embryon philosophers.' Maybe M. Maeterlinck is but an embryon philosopher, one who discourses in Plato's den. But I think we must all recognise the native distinction of his mind, the fastidious delicacy of his taste, his abiding and insatiable love of beauty. What he says, exquisitely enough but perhaps too liberally, of every man—'to every man there come noble thoughts that pass across his heart like great white birds'—is certainly true of himself. Wherefore one may venture to invite people to his book as Heraclitus welcomed guests to his kitchen: 'Enter boldly, for here also there are gods.'

A. B. W.

SILENCE

'SILENCE and Secrecy!' cries Carlyle. 'Altars might still be raised to them (were this an altar-building time) for universal worship. Silence is the element in which great things fashion themselves together, that at length they may emerge, full-formed and majestic, into the daylight of Life, which they are henceforth to rule. Not William the Silent only, but all the considerable men I have known, and the most undiplomatic and unstrategic of these, forbore to babble of what they were creating and projecting. Nay, in thy own mean perplexities, do thou thyself but *hold thy tongue for one day*; on the morrow how much clearer are thy purposes and duties; what wreck and rubbish have these mute workmen within thee swept away, when intrusive noises were shut out! Speech is too often not, as the Frenchman defined it, the art of concealing Thought, but of quite stifling and suspending Thought, so that there is none to conceal. Speech, too, is great, but not the greatest. As the Swiss inscription says: *Sprechen ist Silbern, Schweigen ist goldern* (Speech is silver, Silence is golden); or, as I might rather express it, Speech is of Time, Silence is of Eternity.

'Bees will not work except in darkness; Thought will not work except in Silence; neither will Virtue work except in secrecy.'

IT is idle to think that, by means of words, any real communication can ever pass from one man to another. The lips or the tongue may represent the soul, even as a cipher or a number may represent a picture of Memling; but from the moment that we have *something to say to each other*, we are *compelled* to hold our peace: and if at such times we do not listen to the urgent commands of silence, invisible though they be, we shall have suffered an eternal loss that all the treasures of human wisdom cannot make good; for we shall have let slip the opportunity of listening to another soul, and of giving existence, be it only for an instant, to our own; and many lives there are in which such opportunities do not present themselves twice....

It is only when life is sluggish within us that we speak: only at moments when reality lies far away, and we *do not wish* to be conscious of our brethren. And no sooner do we speak than something warns us that the divine gates are closing. Thus it comes about that we hug silence to us, and are very misers of it; and even the most reckless will not squander it on the first comer. There is an instinct of the superhuman truths within us which warns us that it is dangerous to be silent with one whom we do not wish to know, or do not love: for words may pass between men, but let silence have had its instant of activity, and it will never efface itself; and indeed the true life, the only life that leaves a trace behind, is made up of silence alone. Bethink it well, in that silence to which you must again have recourse, so that it may explain itself, by itself; and if it be granted to you to descend for one moment into your soul, into the depths where the angels dwell, it is not the words spoken by the creature you loved so dearly that you will recall, or the gestures that he made, but it is, above all, the silences that you have lived together that will come back to you: for it is the *quality* of those silences that alone revealed the quality of your love and your souls.

So far I have considered *active* silence only, for there is a *passive* silence, which is the shadow of sleep, of death or non-existence. It is the silence of lethargy, and is even less to be dreaded than speech, so long as it slumbers; but beware lest a sudden incident awake it, for then would its brother, the great active silence, at once rear himself upon his throne. Be on your guard. Two souls would draw near each other: the barriers would fall asunder, the gates fly open, and the life of every day be replaced by a life of deepest earnest, wherein all are defenceless; a life in which laughter dares not show itself, in which there is no obeying, in which nothing can evermore be forgotten....

And it is because we all of us know of this sombre power and its perilous manifestations, that we stand in so deep a dread of silence. We can bear, when need must be, the silence of ourselves, that of isolation: but the silence of many—silence multiplied—and above all the silence of a crowd—these are supernatural burdens, whose inexplicable weight brings dread to the mightiest soul. We spend a goodly portion of our lives in seeking places where silence is not. No sooner have two or three men met than their one thought is to drive away the invisible enemy; and of how many ordinary friendships may it not be said that their only foundation is the common hatred of silence! And if, all efforts notwithstanding, it contrives to steal among a number of men, disquiet will fall upon them, and their restless eyes will wander in the mysterious direction of things unseen: and each man will hurriedly go his way, flying before the intruder: and henceforth they will avoid each other, dreading lest a similar disaster should again befall them, and suspicious as to whether there be not one among them who would treacherously throw open the gate to the enemy....

In the lives of most of us, it will not happen more than twice or thrice that silence is really understood and freely admitted. It is only on the most solemn occasions that the inscrutable guest is welcomed; but, when such come about, there are few who do not make the welcome worthy, for even in the lives of the most wretched there are moments when they know how to act, even as though they knew already that which is known to the gods. Remember the day on which, without fear in your heart, you met your first silence. The dread hour had sounded; silence went before your soul. You saw it rising from the unspeakable abysses of life, from the depths of the inner sea of horror or beauty, and you did not fly.... It was at a home-coming, on the threshold of a departure, in the midst of a great joy, at the pillow of a death-bed, on the approach of a dire misfortune. Bethink you of those moments when all the secret jewels shone forth on you, and the slumbering truths sprung to life, and tell me whether silence, then, was not good and necessary, whether the caresses of the enemy you had so persistently shunned were not truly divine? The kisses of the silence of misfortune—and it is above all at times of misfortune that silence caresses us—can never be forgotten; and therefore it is that those to whom they have come more often than to others are worthier than those others. They alone know, perhaps, how voiceless and unfathomable are the waters on which the fragile shell of daily life reposes: they have approached nearer to God, and the steps they have taken towards the light are steps that can never be lost, for the soul may not rise, perhaps, but it can never sink.... 'Silence, the great Empire of Silence,' says Carlyle again—he who understood so well the empire of the life which holds us—'higher than the stars, deeper than the Kingdom of Death!... Silence, and the great silent men!... Scattered here and there, each in his department; silently thinking, silently working; whom no morning newspaper makes mention of! They are the salt of the earth. A country that has none or few of these is in a bad way. Like a forest which had no *roots*; which had all turned to leaves and boughs; which must soon wither and be no forest.'

But the real silence, which is greater still and more difficult of approach than the material silence of which Carlyle speaks—the real silence is not one of those gods that can desert mankind. It surrounds us on every side; it is the source of the undercurrents of our life; and let one of us but knock, with trembling fingers, at the door of the abyss, it is always by the same attentive silence that this door will be opened.

It is a thing that knows no limit, and before it all men are equal; and the silence of king or slave, in presence of death, or grief, or love, reveals the same features, hides beneath its impenetrable mantle the self-same treasure. For this is the essential silence of our soul, our most inviolable sanctuary, and its secret can never be lost; and, were the first born of men to meet the last inhabitant of the earth, a kindred impulse would sway them, and they would be voiceless in their caresses, in their terror and their tears; a kindred impulse would sway them, and all that could be said without falsehood would call for no spoken word: and, the centuries notwithstanding, there would come to them, at the same moment, as though one cradle had held them both, comprehension of that which the tongue shall not learn to tell before the world ceases....

No sooner are the lips still than the soul awakes, and sets forth on its labours; for silence is an element that is full of surprise, danger and happiness, and in these the soul possesses itself in freedom. If it be indeed your desire to give yourself over to another, be silent; and if you fear being silent with him— unless this fear be the proud uncertainty, or hunger, of the love that yearns for prodigies—fly from him, for your soul knows well how far it may go.

There are men in whose presence the greatest of heroes would not dare to be silent; and even the soul that has nothing to conceal trembles lest another should discover its secret. Some there are that have no silence, and that kill the silence around them, and these are the only creatures that pass through life unperceived. To them it is not given to cross the zone of revelation, the great zone of the firm and faithful light. We cannot conceive what sort of man is he who has never been silent. It is to us as though his soul were featureless. 'We do not know each other yet,' wrote to me one whom I hold dear above all others, 'we have not yet dared to be silent together.' And it was true: already did we love each other so deeply that we shrank from the superhuman ordeal. And each time that silence fell upon us—the angel of the supreme truth, the messenger that brings to the heart the tidings of the unknown—each time did we feel that our souls were craving mercy on their knees, were begging for a few hours more of innocent falsehood, a few hours of ignorance, a few hours of childhood.... And none the less must its hour come. It is the sun of love, and it ripens the fruit of the soul, as the sun of heaven ripens the fruits of the earth. But it is not without cause that men fear it; for none can ever tell what will be the *quality* of the silence which is about to fall upon them. Though all words may be akin, every silence differs from its fellow; and, with rare exceptions, it is an entire destiny that will be governed by the *quality* of this first silence which is descending upon two souls. They blend: we know not where, for the reservoirs of silence lie far above the reservoirs of thought, and the strange resultant brew is either sinisterly bitter or profoundly sweet. Two souls, admirable both and of equal power, may yet give birth to a hostile silence, and wage pitiless war against each other in the darkness; while it may be that the soul of a convict shall go forth and commune in divine silence with the soul of a virgin. The result can never be foretold; all this comes to pass in a heaven that never warns; and therefore it is that the tenderest of lovers will often defer to the last hour of all the solemn entry of the great revealer of the depths of our being....

For they too are well aware—the love that is truly love brings the most frivolous back to life's centre—they too are well aware that all that had gone before was but as children playing outside the gates, and that it is now that the walls are falling and existence lying bare. Their silence will be even as are the gods within them; and if in this first silence, there be not harmony, there can be no love in their souls, for the silence will never change. It may rise or it may fall between two souls, but *its nature* can never alter; and even until the death of the lovers will it retain the form, the attitude and the power that were its own when, for the first time, it came into the room.

As we advance through life, it is more and more brought home to us that nothing takes place that is not in accord with some curious, preconceived design: and of this we never breathe a word, we scarcely dare to let our minds dwell upon it, but of its existence, somewhere above our heads, we are absolutely convinced. The most fatuous of men smiles, at the first encounters, as though he were the accomplice of the destiny of his brethren. And in this domain, even those who can speak the most profoundly realise—they, perhaps, more than others—that words can never express the real, special relationship that exists between two beings. Were I to speak to you at this moment of the gravest things of all—of love, death or destiny—it is not love, death or destiny that I should touch; and, my efforts notwithstanding, there would always remain between us a truth which had not been spoken, which we had not even thought of speaking; and yet it is this truth only, voiceless though it has been, which will have lived with us for an instant, and by which we shall have been wholly absorbed. For that truth was *our truth* as regards death, destiny or love, and it was in silence only that we could perceive it. And nothing save only the silence will have had any importance. 'My sisters,' says a child in the fairy-story, 'you have each of you a secret thought—I wish to know it.' We, too, have something that people wish to know, but it is hidden far above the secret thought—it is our secret silence. But all questions are useless. When our spirit is alarmed, its own agitation becomes a barrier to the second life that lives in this secret; and, would we know what it is that lies hidden there, we must cultivate silence among ourselves, for it is then only that for one instant the eternal flowers unfold their petals, the mysterious flowers whose form and colour are ever changing in harmony with the soul that is by their side. As gold and silver are weighed in pure water, so does the soul test its weight in silence, and the words that we let fall have no meaning apart from the silence that wraps them round. If I tell some one that I love him—as I may have told a hundred others—my words will convey nothing to him; but the silence which will ensue, if I do indeed love him, will make clear in what depths lie the roots of my love, and will in its turn give birth to a conviction, that shall itself be silent; and in the course of a lifetime, this silence and this conviction will never again be the same....

Is it not silence that determines and fixes the savour of love? Deprived of it, love would lose its eternal essence and perfume. Who has not known those silent moments which separated the lips to reunite the souls? It is these that we must ever seek. There is no silence more docile than the silence of love, and it is indeed the only one that we may claim for ourselves alone. The other great silences, those of death, grief, or destiny, do not belong to us. They come towards us at their own hour, following in the track of events, and those whom they do not meet need not reproach themselves. But we can all go forth to meet the silences of love. They lie in wait for us, night and day, at our threshold, and are no less beautiful than their brothers. And it is thanks to them that those who have seldom wept may know the life of the soul almost as intimately as those to whom much grief has come: and therefore it is that such of us as have loved deeply have learnt many secrets that are unknown to others: for thousands and thousands of things quiver in silence on the lips of true friendship and love, that are not to be found in the silence of other lips, to which friendship and love are unknown....

THE AWAKENING OF THE SOUL

A TIME will come, perhaps—and many things there are that herald its approach—a time will come perhaps when our souls will know of each other without the intermediary of the senses. Certain it is that there passes not a day but the soul adds to its ever-widening domain. It is very much nearer to our visible self, and takes a far greater part in all our actions, than was the case two or three centuries ago. A spiritual epoch is perhaps upon us; an epoch to which a certain number of analogies are found in history. For there are periods recorded, when the soul, in obedience to unknown laws, seemed to rise to the very surface of humanity, whence it gave clearest evidence of its existence and of its power. And this existence and this power reveal themselves in countless ways, diverse and unforeseen. It would seem, at moments such as these, as though humanity were on the point of struggling from beneath the crushing burden of matter that weighs it down. A spiritual influence is abroad that soothes and comforts; and the sternest, direst laws of Nature yield here and there. Men are nearer to themselves, nearer to their brothers; in the look of their eyes, in the love of their hearts, there is deeper earnestness and tenderer fellowship. Their understanding of women, children, animals, plants—nay, of all things—becomes more pitiful and more profound. The statues, paintings and writings that these men have left us may perhaps not be perfect, but, none the less does there dwell therein a secret power, an indescribable grace, held captive and imperishable for ever. A mysterious brotherhood and love must have shone forth from the eyes of these men; and signs of a life that we cannot explain are everywhere, vibrating by the side of the life of every day.

Such knowledge as we possess of ancient Egypt induces us to believe that she passed through one of these spiritual epochs. At a very remote period in the history of India, the soul must have drawn very near to the surface of life, to a point, indeed, that it has never since touched; and unto this day strange phenomena owe their being to the recollection, or lingering remnants, of its almost immediate presence. Many other similar moments there have been, when the spiritual element seemed to be struggling far down in the depths of humanity, like a drowning man battling for life beneath the waters of a great river. Bethink you of Persia, for instance, of Alexandria, and the two mystic centuries of the Middle Ages.

On the other hand, there have been centuries in which purest intellect and beauty reigned supreme, though the soul lay unrevealed. Thus it was far from Greece and Rome, and from the seventeenth and eighteenth centuries in France. (As regards this last, however, we may perhaps be speaking only of the surface; for in its depths many mysteries lie concealed—we must remember Claude de Saint-Martin, Cagliostro—who is passed over too lightly—Pascalis, and many others besides.) Something is lacking, we know not what; barriers are stretched across the secret passages; the eyes of beauty are sealed. Well-nigh hopeless, indeed, is the attempt to convey this in words, or to explain why the atmosphere of divinity and fatality that enwraps the Greek dramas does not seem to us to be the true atmosphere of the soul. Majestic and all-abiding as is the mystery that lingers on the horizon of these matchless tragedies, it is yet not the pitiful, brotherly mystery, quickened into profound activity, that we find in other works less great and less beautiful. And to come nearer to our own time—though Racine may indeed be the unerring poet of the woman's heart, who would dare to claim for him that he has ever taken one step towards her soul? What can you tell me of the soul of Andromache, of Britannicus? Racine's characters have no knowledge of themselves beyond the words by which they express themselves, and not one of these words can pierce the dykes that keep back the sea. His men and women are alone, fearfully alone, on the surface of a planet that no longer revolves in the heavens. If they were to be silent, they would cease to be. They have no *invisible principle*, and one might almost believe that some isolating substance had crept between their spirit and themselves, between the life which has its roots in every created thing and that which, for one fleeting moment, brushes against a passion, a grief or a hope. Truly there are centuries in which the soul lies dormant and slumbers undisturbed.

But to-day it is clearly making a mighty effort. Its manifestations are everywhere, and they are strangely urgent, pressing, imperious even, as though the order had been given, and no time must be lost. It must be preparing for a decisive struggle; and none can foretell the issues that may be dependent on the result, be this victory or flight. Perhaps never to this day has it enlisted in its service such diverse, irresistible forces. It is as though an invisible wall hemmed it in, and one knows not whether it be quivering in its death-throb or quickened by a new life. I will say nothing of the occult powers, of which signs are everywhere—of magnetism, telepathy, levitation, the unsuspected properties of radiating matter, and countless other phenomena that are battering down the door of orthodox science. These things are known of all men, and can easily be verified. And truly they may well be the merest bagatelle by the side of the vast upheaval that is actually in progress, for the soul is like a dreamer, enthralled by sleep, who struggles with all his might to move an arm or raise an eyelid.

Other regions there are where its action is even more effective, though the crowd there is less regardful, and none but trained eyes can see. Does it not seem as though the supreme cry of the soul were at last about to pierce the dense clouds of error that still envelop it in music? Do not certain pictures by foreign painters reveal the sacred majesty of an invisible presence, as it never has been revealed before? Are there not masterpieces in literature that are illumined by a flame which differs in its very essence from the strangest beacon-fires that lit up the writings of bygone days? A transformation of silence—strange and inexplicable—is upon us, and the reign of the *positive sublime*, absolute to this day, seems destined to be overthrown. I will not linger on this subject, for the time has not yet come for lucid discussion of these things; but I feel that a more pressing offer of spiritual freedom has rarely been made to mankind. Nay, there are moments when it bears the semblance of an ultimatum; and therefore does it behove us to neglect nothing, but indeed with all eagerness to accept this imperious invitation, that is like unto the dream that is lost for ever, unless instantaneously seized. We must be heedful; it is not without fit reason that our soul bestirs itself.

Though it be perhaps from the table-lands of speculative thought that this agitation is the most clearly to be noted, yet may there well be signs of it in the most ordinary paths of life, unsuspected of any; for not a flower opens on the hill-top but at length it falls into the valley. Has it fallen already? I know not. But this much at least is abundantly proved to us, that in the work-a-day lives of the very humblest of men, spiritual phenomena manifest themselves—mysterious, direct workings, that bring soul nearer to soul; and of all this we can find no record in former times. And the reason must surely be that these things were not so clearly evident then: for at every period there have been men who penetrated to the innermost recesses of life, to its most secret affinities: and all that they learned of the heart, the soul and the spirit of their epoch has been handed down to us. It may well be that similar influences were at work even in those times; but they could not have been as universal, as active and vigorous as they are to-day, nor could they have sunk so deep into the very life-springs of the race; for in that case, they had surely not escaped the notice of those sages, and been passed by in silence. And I do not refer now to 'scientific spiritism,' or its telepathic phenomena, to 'materialisation,' or other manifestations that I have enumerated above: but to the incidents, the interventions, that occur unceasingly in the dreariest lives of all, those of the men who are the most forgetful of their eternal rights. Also must it be borne in mind that we are not considering the ordinary text-book psychology—which concerns itself only with such spiritual phenomena as are the most closely interwoven with the material, having indeed usurped the beautiful name of Psyche—the psychology of which I speak is transcendental, and throws light on the direct relationship that exists between soul and soul, and on the *sensibility* as well as the *extraordinary presence* of the soul. It is a science that is in its infancy; but by it shall men be taken a full step higher, and very speedily shall it dismiss for ever the elementary psychology that has been dominant to this day.

This 'immediate' psychology is descending from the mountain tops, and laying siege to the humblest of valleys; and even in the most mediocre of writings is its presence to be felt. And indeed, than this, nothing could prove more clearly that the pressure of the soul has increased among mankind, and that its mysterious influence is diffusing itself among the people. But we are now drawing near to things that are well-nigh unspeakable, and such examples as one can give are necessarily ordinary and incomplete. The following are elementary and readily appreciable. In former days, if there was question, for a moment, of a presentiment, of the strange impression produced by a chance meeting or a look, of a decision that the unknown side of human reason had governed, of an intervention, or a force, inexplicable and yet understood, of the secret laws of sympathy and antipathy, of elective and instinctive affinities, of the overwhelming influence of the thing that had not been spoken—in former days, these problems would have been carelessly passed by, and, besides, it was but seldom that they intruded themselves upon the serenity of the thinker. They seemed to come about by the merest chance. That they are ever pressing upon life, unceasingly and with prodigious force—this was unsuspected of all—and the philosopher hastened back to familiar studies of passion, and of incident that floated on the surface.

These spiritual phenomena, to which, in bygone days, even the greatest and wisest of our brothers scarcely gave a thought, are to-day being earnestly studied by the very smallest; and herein are we shown once again that the human soul is a plant of matchless unity, whose branches, when the hour is come, all burst into blossom together. The peasant, to whom the power of expressing that which lies in his soul should suddenly be given, would at this moment pour forth ideas that were not yet in the soul of Racine. And thus it is that men of a genius much inferior to that of Shakespeare or Racine have yet had revealed to them glimpses of a secretly luminous life, whose outer crust, alone, had come within the ken of those masters. For, however great the soul, it avails not that it should wander in isolation through space or time. Unaided, it can do but little. It is the flower of the multitude. When the spiritual sea is storm-tossed, and its whole surface restless and troubled, then is the moment ripe for the mighty soul to appear; but if it come at time of slumber, its utterance will be but of the dreams of sleep. Hamlet—to take the most illustrious of all examples—Hamlet, at Elsinore—at every moment does he advance to the very brink of awakening; and yet, though his haggard face be damp with icy sweat, there are words that he cannot utter, words that to-day would doubtless flow readily from his lips, because the soul of the passer-by, be he tramp or thief, would be there to help him. For, in truth, it would seem that already there are fewer veils that enwrap the soul; and were

Hamlet now to look into the eyes of his mother, or of Claudius, there would be revealed to him the things that, then, he did not know. Is it thoroughly clear to you—this is one of the strangest, most disquieting of truths—is it thoroughly clear to you that, if there be evil in your heart, your mere presence will probably proclaim it to-day a hundred times more clearly than would have been the case two or three centuries ago? Is it fully borne home to you that if you have perchance this morning done anything that shall have brought sadness to a single human being, the peasant, with whom you are about to talk of the rain or the storm, will know of it—his soul will have been warned even before his hand has thrown open the door? Though you assume the face of a saint, a hero or a martyr, the eye of the passing child will not greet you with the same unapproachable smile if there lurk within you an evil thought, an injustice, or a brother's tears. A hundred years ago the soul of that child would perhaps have passed, unheeding, by the side of yours....

Truly it is becoming difficult to cherish hatred, envy, or treachery in one's heart, secure from observation; for the souls even of the most indifferent are incessantly keeping vigil around us. Our ancestors have not spoken of these things, and we realise that the life in which we bestir ourselves is quite other than that which they have depicted. Have they deceived us, or did they not know? Signs and words no longer count for anything, and in mystic circles it is the mere presence that decides almost all.

Even the ancient 'will-power'—the logical will-power that men have professed to understand so well—even this is being transformed in its turn, and moulded beneath the pressure of mighty, deep searching, inexplicable laws. The last refuges are disappearing, and men are drawing closer to each other. Far above words and acts do they judge their fellows—nay, far above thought—for that which they see, though they understand it not, lies well beyond the domain of thought. And this is one of the great signs by which the spiritual periods I spoke of before shall be known. It is felt on all sides that the conditions of work-a-day life are changing, and the youngest of us already differ entirely in speech and action from the men of the preceding generation. A mass of useless conventions, habits, pretences, and intermediaries are being swept into the gulf; and it is by the invisible alone that, though we know it not, nearly all of us judge each other. If I enter your room for the first time you will not pronounce the secret sentence that, according to the laws of practical psychology, each man pronounces in the presence of his fellow. In vain shall you try to tell me whither you have been to learn who I am, but you shall come back to me, bearing the weight of unspeakable certitudes. Your father, perhaps, would have judged me otherwise, and would have been mistaken. We can but believe that man will soon touch man, and that the atmosphere will change. 'Have we,' asks Claude de Saint-Martin, the great 'unknown philosopher,' 'have we advanced one step further on the radiant path of enlightenment, that leads to the simplicity of men?' Let us wait in silence: perhaps ere long we shall be conscious of 'the murmur of the gods.'

THE PRE-DESTINED

THEY are known to most men, and there are few mothers who have not seen them. Perhaps they are as inevitable as life's sorrows; and the men among whom they dwell become the better for the knowledge of them, and the sadder, and the more gentle.

They are strange. As children, life seems nearer to them than to other children; they appear to suspect nothing, and yet is there in their eyes so profound a certainty that we feel they must know all, that there must have been evenings when they found time to tell themselves their secret. At the moment when their brothers are still groping their way blindly in the mysterious land between birth and life, they have already understood; they are erect, ready with hand and soul. In all haste, but wisely and with minute care, do they prepare themselves to live; and this very haste is a sign upon which mothers, the discreet, unsuspected confidants of all that cannot be told, can scarce bring themselves to look.

Their stay among us is often so short that we are unconscious of their presence; they go away without saying a word, and are for ever unknown to us. But others there are who linger for a moment, who look at us with an eager smile, and seem to be on the point of confessing that they know all; and then, towards their twentieth year, they leave us, hurriedly, muffling their footsteps, as though they had just discovered that they had chosen the wrong dwelling-place, and had been about to pass their lives among men whom they did not know.

They themselves say but little, and there is a cloud that falls around them at the moment when men seem on the point of touching them, or when hurt has been done them. Some days there are when they seem to be of us, and among us, but a sudden evening comes and they are so far away that we dare not look at them, or ask a question. It is as though they were on life's further shore, and the feeling rushes in upon us that now, at last, the hour has come for affirming that which is graver, deeper, more human, more real than friendship, pity or love; for saying the thing that is piteously flapping its wings at the back of our throat, and craving for utterance—the thing that our ignorance crushes, that we never have said, that we never shall say, for so many lives are spent in silence! And time rushes on; and who is there of us but has lingered and waited till it was too late, and there was no one to listen to his words?

Why have they come to us—why do they go so soon? Is it only that we may be convinced of the utter aimlessness of life? It is a mystery that ever eludes us, and all our searchings are vain. I have often seen these things happen;

one day they were so near to me that I scarcely knew was it myself or another whom they concerned....

For it was thus that my brother died. And though he alone had heard the warning whisper, be it ever so unconsciously—for from his earliest days he had concealed the message of disease within him—yet surely had the knowledge of what was to come been borne in upon us also. What are the signs that set apart the creatures for whom dire events lie in wait? Nothing is visible, and yet all is revealed. They are afraid of us, for that we are ever crying out to them of our knowledge, struggle against it as we may; and when we are with them, they can see that, in our hearts, we are oppressed by their destiny. Something there is that we hide from most men, and we ourselves are ignorant of what this thing may be. Strange secrets of life and death pass between two creatures who meet for the first time; and many other secrets besides, nameless to this day, but which at once thrust their impress upon our bearing, our features, the look of our eyes; and even while we press the hand of our friend, our soul will have soared perhaps beyond the confines of this life. It may be that when two men are together, they are unconscious of any hidden thoughts, but there are things that lie deeper, and are far more imperious, than thought. We are not the lords of these unfathomable gifts; and we are ever betraying the presence of the prophet to whom speech is not given. We are never the same with others as when we are alone; we are different, even, when we are in the dark with them, and the look in our eyes changes as the past or future flashes before us; and therefore it is that, though we know it not, we are ever watchful and on our guard. When we meet those who are not to live long, we are only conscious of the fate that is hanging over them; we see nothing else. If they could they would deceive us, so that they might the more readily deceive themselves. They do all in their power to mislead us; they imagine that their eager smile, their burning interest in life, will conceal the truth; but none the less does the event already loom large before us, and seem indeed to be the mainstay, nay, the very reason of their existence. Death has again betrayed them, and they realise, in bitter sadness, that nothing is hidden from us, that there are certain voices that cannot be still.

Who can tell us of the power which events possess—whether they issue from us, or whether we owe our being to them? Do we attract them, or are we attracted by them? Do we mould them, or do they mould us? Are they always unerring in their course? Why do they come to us like the bee to the hive, like the dove to the cote; and where do they find a resting-place when we are not there to meet them? Whence is it that they come to us; and why are they shaped in our image, as though they were our brothers? Are their workings in the past or in the future; and are the more powerful of them those that are no longer, or those that are not yet? Is it to-day or to-morrow that moulds us? Do we not all spend the greater part of our lives under the shadow of an event that has not yet come to pass? I have noticed the same grave gestures, the footsteps that seemed to tend towards a goal that was all too near, the presentiments that chilled the blood, the fixed, immovable look—I have noticed all these in the men, even, whose end was to come about by accident, the men on whom death would suddenly seize from without. And yet were they as eager as their brethren, who bore the seeds of death within them. Their faces were the same. To them, too, life was fraught with more seriousness than to those who were to live their full span. The same careful, silent watchfulness marked their actions. They had no time to lose; they had to be in readiness at the same hour; so completely had this event, which no prophet could have foretold, become the very life of their life.

It is death that is the guide of our life, and our life has no goal but death. Our death is the mould into which our life flows: it is death that has shaped our features. Of the dead alone should portraits be painted, for it is only they who are truly themselves, and who, for one instant, stand revealed even as they are. What life is there but becomes radiant when the pure, cold, simple light falls on it at the last hour? It is, perhaps, the same light that floats around children's faces when they smile at us; and the silence that steals over us then is akin to that of the chamber where there will be peace for evermore. I have known many whom the same death was leading by the hand, and when my memory dwells upon them I see a band of children, of youths and maidens, who seem to be all coming forth from the same house. A strange fraternity already unites them: it may be that they recognise each other by birth-marks we cannot discover, that they furtively exchange solemn signals of silence. They are the eager children of precocious death. At school we were vaguely conscious of them. They seemed to be at the same time seeking and avoiding each other, like people who are afflicted with the same infirmity. They were to be seen together, in remote corners of the garden, under the trees. Their mysterious smile flew fitfully across their lips, and there lurked a gravity beneath, a curious fear lest a secret should escape. Silence would almost always fall upon them, when those who were to live drew near. Were they already speaking of the event, or did they know that the event was speaking through them, and in their despite? Were they forming a circle round it, and trying to keep it hidden from indifferent eyes? There were times when they seemed to be looking down upon us from a lofty tower; and, for all that we were the stronger, we dared not molest them. For truly there is nothing that can ever be really hidden; and whosoever meets me knows all that I have done and shall do, all that I have thought and do think—nay, he knows the very day on which I shall die; but the means of telling what he knows is not given to him, though he speak never so softly, and whisper to his heart. We pass heedlessly by the side of all that our hands cannot touch; and perhaps too great a knowledge would be ours if all that we do know were revealed to us. Our real life is not the life we live, and we feel that our deepest, nay, our most intimate thoughts are quite apart from ourselves, for we are other than our thoughts and our dreams. And it is only at special moments—it may be by merest accident—that we live our own life. Will the day ever dawn when we shall be what we are?... In the meanwhile, we felt that they were strangers in our midst. A sensation of awe crept into our life. Sometimes they would walk with us along the corridor, or in the courtyard, and we could scarcely keep pace with them. Sometimes they would join us at our games, and the game would no longer be the same. There were some who could not find their brethren. They would wander in solitude in our midst, while we played and shouted: they had no friends among those who were not about to die. And yet we loved them, and the deepest friendliness shone from their eyes. What was there that divided us from them? What is there that divides us all? What is this sea of mysteries in whose depths we have our being? The love that we felt was the love that seeks not to express itself, because it is not of this world. It is a love, perhaps, that cannot be put to the proof; it may seem feeble, uncertain, and the smallest, most ordinary friendship may appear to triumph over it—but none the less does its life lie deeper than our life, and none the less, notwithstanding its seeming indifference, is it reserved for a time when doubt and uncertainty shall be no longer....

Its voice does not make itself heard now because its moment for speaking has not yet come; and it is never those whom we enfold in our arms that we love the most deeply. For there is a side of life—and it is the best, the purest, the noblest side—which never blends with the ordinary life, and the eyes even of lovers themselves can seldom pierce through the masonry that is built up of silence and love....

Or was it that we avoided them, because, though younger than ourselves, they still were our elders?... Did we know that they were not of our age, and did we fear them, as though they were sitting in judgment upon us? A curious steadfastness already lurked in their eyes; and if, in our moments of agitation, their glance rested upon us, it would soothe and comfort us, we knew not why, and there would be an instant of strangest silence. We would turn round: they were watching us and smiling gravely. There were two for whom a violent death was lying in wait—I remember their faces well. But almost all were timid, and tried to pass by unperceived. They were weighed down by some deadly sense of shame, they seemed to be ever beseeching forgiveness for a fault they knew not of, but which was near at hand. They came towards us and our eyes met; we drew asunder, silently, and all was clear to us, though we knew nothing.

MYSTIC MORALITY

IT is only too evident that the invisible agitations of the kingdoms within us are arbitrarily set on foot by the thoughts we shelter. Our myriad intuitions are the veiled queens who steer our course through life, though we have no words in which to speak of them. How strangely do we diminish a thing as soon as we try to express it in words! We believe we have dived down to the most unfathomable depths, and when we reappear on the surface, the drop of water that glistens on our trembling finger-tips no longer resembles the sea from which it came. We believe we have discovered a grotto that is stored with bewildering treasure; we come back to the light of day, and the gems we have brought are false—mere pieces of glass—and yet does the treasure shine on, unceasingly, in the darkness! There is something between ourselves and our soul that nothing can penetrate; and there are moments, says Emerson, 'in which we court suffering, in the hope that here at least we shall find reality, sharp peaks and edges of truth.'

I have said elsewhere that the souls of mankind seemed to be drawing nearer to each other, and even if this be not a statement that can be proved, it is none the less based upon deep-rooted, though obscure, convictions. It is indeed difficult to advance facts in its support, for facts are nothing but the laggards, the spies and camp followers of the great forces we cannot see. But surely there are moments when we seem to feel, more deeply than did our fathers before us, that we are not in the presence of ourselves alone. Neither those who believe in a God, nor those who disbelieve, are found to act in themselves as though they were sure of being alone. We are watched, we are under strictest supervision, and it comes from elsewhere than the indulgent darknesses of each man's conscience! Perhaps the spiritual vases are less closely sealed now than in bygone days, perhaps more power has come to the waves of the sea within us? I know not: all that we can state with certainty is that we no longer attach the same importance to a certain number of traditional faults, but this is in itself a token of a spiritual victory.

It would seem as though our code of morality were changing—advancing with timid steps towards loftier regions that cannot yet be seen. And the moment has perhaps come when certain new questions should be asked. What would happen, let us say, if our soul were suddenly to take visible shape, and were compelled to advance into the midst of her assembled sisters, stripped of all her veils, but laden with her most secret thoughts, and dragging behind her the most mysterious, inexplicable acts of her life? Of what would she be ashamed? Which are the things she fain would hide? Would she, like a bashful maiden, cloak beneath her long hair the numberless sins of the flesh? She knows not of them, and those sins have never come near her. They were committed a thousand miles from her throne; and the soul even of the prostitute would pass unsuspectingly through the crowd, with the transparent smile of the child in her eyes. She has not interfered, she was living her life where the light fell on her, and it is this life only that she can recall.

Are there any sins or crimes of which she could be guilty? Has she betrayed, deceived, lied? Has she inflicted suffering or been the cause of tears? Where was she while this man delivered over his brother to the enemy? Perhaps, far away from him, she was sobbing; and from that moment she will have become more beautiful and more profound. She will feel no shame for that which she has not done; she can remain pure in the midst of terrible murder. Often, she will transform into inner radiance all the evil wrought before her. These things are governed by an invisible principle; and hence, doubtless, has arisen the inexplicable indulgence of the gods.

And our indulgence, too. Strive as we may, we are bound to pardon; and when death, 'the great Conciliator,' has passed by, is there one of us who does not fall on his knees and silently, with every token of forgiveness, bend over the departing soul? When I stand before the rigid body of my bitterest enemy: when I look upon the pale lips that slandered me, the sightless eyes that so often brought the tears to mine, the cold hands that may have wrought me so much wrong—do you imagine that I can still think of revenge? Death has come and atoned for all. I have no grievance against the soul of the man before me. Instinctively do I recognise that it soars high above the gravest faults and the cruellest wrongs (and how admirable and full of significance is this instinct!). If there linger still a regret within me, it is not that I am unable to inflict suffering in my turn, but it is perhaps that my love was not great enough and that my forgiveness has come too late....

One might almost believe that these things were already understood by us, deep down in our soul. We do not judge our fellows by their acts—nay, not even by their most secret thoughts; for these are not always undiscernible, and we go far beyond the undiscernible. A man shall have committed crimes reputed to be the vilest of all, and yet it may be that even the blackest of these shall not have tarnished, for one single moment, the breath of fragrance and ethereal purity that surrounds his presence; while at the approach of a philosopher or martyr our soul may be steeped in unendurable gloom. It may happen that a saint or hero shall choose his friend from among men whose faces bear the stamp of every degraded thought; and that, by the side of others, whose brows are radiant with lofty and magnanimous dreams, he shall not feel a 'human and brotherly atmosphere' about him. What tidings do these things bring us? And wherein lies their significance? Are there laws deeper than those by which deeds and thoughts are governed? What are the things we have learned and why do we always act in accordance with rules that none ever mention, but which are the only rules that cannot err? For it may be boldly declared that, appearances notwithstanding, neither hero nor saint has chosen wrongly. They have but obeyed, and even though the saint be deceived and sold by the man he has preferred, still will there abide with him something imperishable, something by which he shall know that he was right and that he has nothing to regret. The soul will ever remember that the other soul was pure....

When we venture to move the mysterious stone that covers these mysteries, the heavily charged air surges up from the gulf, and words and thoughts fall around us like poisoned flies. Even our inner life seems trivial by the side of these unchanging deepnesses. When the angels stand before you, will you glory in never having sinned; and is there not an inferior innocence? When Jesus read the wretched thoughts of the Pharisees who surrounded the paralytic of Capernaum, are you sure that as He looked at them, He judged their soul—and condemned it—without beholding, far away behind their thoughts, a brightness that was perhaps everlasting? And would He be a God if His condemnation were irrevocable? But why does He speak as though He lingered on the threshold? Will the basest thought or the noblest inspiration leave a mark on the diamond's surface? What god, that is indeed on the heights, but must smile at our gravest faults, as we smile at the puppies on the hearthrug? And what god would he be who would not smile? If you become truly pure, do you think you will try to conceal the petty motives of your great actions from the eyes of the angels before you? And yet are there not in us many things that will look pitiful indeed before the gods assembled on the mountain? Surely that must be, and our soul knows full well that it will have to render its account. It lives in silence, and the hand of a great judge is ever upon it, though his sentences are beyond our ken. What accounts will it have to render? Where shall we find the code of morality that can enlighten us? Is there a mysterious morality that holds sway in regions far beyond our thoughts? Are our most secret desires only the helpless satellites of a central star, that is hidden from our eyes? Does a transparent tree exist within us, and are all our actions and all our virtues only its ephemeral flowers and leaves? Indeed we know not what are the wrongs that our soul can commit, nor what there can be that should make us blush before a higher intelligence or before another soul; and yet which of us feels that he is pure and does not dread the coming of the judge? And where is there a soul that is not afraid of another soul?

*

Here, we are no longer in the well-known valleys of human and psychic life. We find ourselves at the door of the third enclosure: that of the divine life of the mystics. We have to grope timidly, and make sure of every footstep, as we cross the threshold. And even when the threshold is crossed, where shall certainty be found? Where shall we discover those marvellous laws that we are perhaps constantly disobeying: laws of whose existence our conscience is ignorant, though our soul has been warned? Whence comes the shadow of a mysterious transgression that at times creeps over our life and makes it so hard to bear? What are the great spiritual sins of which we can be guilty? Will it be our shame to have striven against our soul, or is there an invisible struggle between our soul and God? And is this struggle so strangely silent that not even a whisper floats on the air? Is there a moment when we can hear the queen whose lips are sealed? She is sternly silent when events do but float on the surface; but there are others perhaps that we scarcely heed, which have their roots deep down in eternity. Some one is dying, some one looks at you, or cries, some other is coming towards you for the first time, or an enemy is passing by—may she not perhaps whisper then? And if you listened to her, while already you no longer love, in the future, the friend at whom you now are smiling? But all this is nothing, and is not even near to the outer lights of the abyss. One cannot speak of these things—the solitude is too great. 'In truth,' says Novalis, 'it is only here and there that the soul bestirs itself; when will it move as a whole, and when will humanity begin to feel with one conscience?' It is only when this takes place that some will learn. We must wait in patience till this superior conscience be gradually, slowly, formed. Then perhaps some one will come to whom it will be given to express what it is that we all feel as regards this side of the soul, which is like to the face of the moon, that none have perceived since the world began.

ON WOMEN

IN these domains also are the laws unknown. Far above our heads, in the very centre of the sky, shines the star of our destined love; and it is in the atmosphere of that star, and illumined by its rays, that every passion that stirs us will come to life, even to the end. And though we choose to right or to left of us, on the heights or in the shallows; though, in our struggle to break through the enchanted circle that is drawn around all the acts of our life, we do violence to the instinct that moves us, and try our hardest to choose against the choice of destiny, yet shall the woman we elect always have come to us straight from the unvarying star. And if, like Don Juan, we take a thousand and three to our embraces, still shall we find, on that evening when arms fall asunder and lips disunite, that it is always the same woman, good or bad, tender or cruel, loving or faithless, that is standing before us.

For indeed we can never emerge from the little circle of light that destiny traces about our footsteps; and one might almost believe that the extent and the hue of this impassable ring are known even to the men who are furthest from us. It is the tinge of its spiritual rays that they perceive first of all, and therefore will it come about that they will either smilingly hold out their hand to us or draw it back in fear. A superior atmosphere exists, in which we all know each other; and there is a mysterious truth—deeper far than the material truth—to which we at once have recourse, when we try to form a conception of a stranger. Have we not all experienced these things, which take place in the impenetrable regions of almost astral humanity? If you receive a letter that has come to you from some far-away island lost in the heart of the ocean, from a stranger whose very existence was unknown to you, are you quite sure that it is really a stranger who has written to you? And, as you read, do not certain deep-rooted, infallible convictions—to which ordinary convictions are as nothing—come to you concerning this soul that is thus meeting yours, in spheres known to the gods alone? And, further, can you not understand that this soul, that was dreaming of yours, heedless of time or space, that this soul, too, had certitudes akin to your own? Strangest recognitions take place on all sides, and we cannot hide our existence. Perhaps nothing brings into broader daylight the subtle bonds that interconnect all mankind than the little mysteries which attend the exchange of a few letters between two strangers. This is perhaps one of the minute crevices—wretchedly insignificant, no doubt, but so few there are that the faintest glimmer of light must content us—this is perhaps one of the minute crevices in the door of darkness, through which we are allowed to peer for one instant, and so conceive to ourselves what must be taking place in the grotto of treasures, undiscovered to this day. Look through the passive correspondence of any man, and you shall find in it an astonishing unity. I know neither of the two men who have written to me this morning, yet am I already aware that my reply to the one will differ in its essence from my reply to the other. I have caught a glimpse of the invisible. And, in my turn, when some one, whom I have never seen, writes to me, I know quite well that had he been writing to the friend who is now before me, his letter had not been exactly the same. A difference will there always be—but it is spiritual and intangible. It is the invisible signal of the soul that salutes its fellow. Doubtless must there be regions outside our ken where none are unknown; a common fatherland whither we may go and meet each other, and whence the return knows no hardship.

And it is in this common fatherland also that we chose the women we loved, wherefore it is that we cannot have erred, nor can they have erred either. The kingdom of love is, before all else, the great kingdom of certitude, for it is within its bounds that the soul is possessed of the utmost leisure. There, truly, they have naught to do but to recognise each other, offer deepest admiration, and ask their questions—tearfully, like the maid who has found the sister she had lost—while, far away from them, arm links itself in arm and breaths are mingling.... At last has a moment come when they can smile and live their own life—for a truce has been called in the stern routine of daily existence—and it is perhaps from the heights of this smile and these ineffable glances that springs the mysterious perfume that pervades love's dreariest moments, that preserves for ever the memory of the time when the lips first met....

Of the true, pre-destined love alone, do I speak here. When Fate sends forth the woman it has chosen for us—sends her forth from the fastnesses of the great spiritual cities in which we, all unconsciously, dwell, and she awaits us at the crossing of the road we have to traverse when the hour is come—we are warned at the first glance. Some there are who attempt to force the hand of Fate. Wildly pressing down their eyelids, so as not to see that which had to be seen—struggling with all their puny strength against the eternal forces—they will contrive perhaps to cross the road and go towards another, sent thither but not for them. But, strive as they may, they will not succeed in 'stirring up the dead waters that lie in the great tarn of the future.' Nothing will happen; the pure force will not descend from the heights, and those wasted hours and kisses will never become part of the real hours and kisses of their life....

There are times when destiny shuts her eyes, but she knows full well that, when evening falls, we shall return to her, and that the last word must be hers. She may shut her eyes, but the time till she re-open them is time that is lost....

It would seem that women are more largely swayed by destiny than ourselves. They submit to its decrees with far more simplicity; nor is there sincerity in the resistance they offer. They are still nearer to God, and yield themselves with less reserve to the pure workings of the mystery. And therefore is it, doubtless, that all the incidents in our life in which they take part seem to bring us nearer to what might almost be the very fountain-head of destiny. It is above all when by their side that moments come, unexpectedly, when a 'clear presentiment' flashes across us, a presentiment of a life that does not always seem parallel to the life we know of. They lead us close to the gates of our being. May it not be during one of those profound moments, when his head is pillowed on a woman's breast, that the hero learns to know the strength and steadfastness of his star? And indeed will any true sentiment of the future ever come to the man who has not had his resting-place in a woman's heart?

Yet again do we enter the troubled circles of the higher conscience. Ah! how true it is that, here, too, 'the so-called psychology is a hobgoblin that has usurped, in the sanctuary itself, the place reserved for the veritable images of the gods.' For it is not the surface that always concerns us—nay, nor is it even the deepest of hidden thoughts. Do you imagine that love knows only of thoughts, and acts, and words, and that the soul never emerges from its dungeon? Do I need to be told whether she whom I take in my arms to-day is jealous or faithful, gay or sad, sincere or treacherous? Do you think that these wretched words can attain the heights whereon our souls repose and where our destiny fulfils itself in silence? What care I whether she speak of rain or jewels, of pins or feathers; what care I though she appear not to understand? Do you think that it is for a sublime word I thirst when I feel that a soul is gazing into my soul? Do I not know that the most beautiful of thoughts dare not raise their heads when the mysteries confront them? I am ever standing at the sea-shore; and, were I Plato, Pascal, or Michael Angelo, and the woman I loved merely telling me of her earrings, the words I would say and the words she would say would appear but the same as they floated on the waves of the fathomless inner sea, that each of us would be contemplating in the other. Let but my very loftiest thought be weighed in the scale of life or love, it will not turn the balance against the three little words that the maid who loves me shall have whispered of her silver bangles, her pearl necklace, or her trinkets of glass....

It is we who do not understand, for that we never rise above the earth-level of our intellect. Let us but ascend to the first snows of the mountain, and all inequalities are levelled by the purifying hand of the horizon that opens before us. What difference then between a pronouncement of Marcus Aurelius and the words of the child complaining of the cold? Let us be humble, and learn to distinguish between accident and essence. Let not 'sticks that float' cause us to forget the prodigies of the gulf. The most glorious thoughts and the most degraded ideas can no more ruffle the eternal surface of our soul than, amidst the stars of Heaven, Himalaya or precipice can alter the surface of the earth. A look, a kiss, and the certainty of a great invisible presence: all is said; and I know that she who is by my side is my equal....

But truly this equal is admirable, and strange; and, when love comes to her, even the lowest of wantons possesses that which we never have, inasmuch as, in her thoughts, love is always eternal. Therefore it is, perhaps, that, besides their primitive instincts, all women have communications with the unknown that are denied to us. Great is the distance that separates the best of men from the treasures of the second boundary; and, when a solemn moment of life demands a jewel from this treasure, they no longer remember the paths that thither lead, and vainly offer to the imperious, undeceivable circumstance the false trinkets that their intellect has fashioned. But the woman never forgets the path that leads to the centre of her being; and no matter whether I find her in opulence or in poverty, in ignorance or in fulness of knowledge, in shame or in glory, do I but whisper one word that has truly come forth from the virgin depths of my soul, she will retrace her footsteps along the mysterious paths that she has never forgotten, and without a moment's hesitation will she bring back to me, from out her inexhaustible stores of love, a word, a look, or a gesture that shall be no less pure than my own. It is as though her soul were ever within call; for by day and night is she prepared to give answer to the loftiest appeals from another soul; and the ransom of the poorest is undistinguishable from the ransom of a queen....

With reverence must we draw near to them, be they lowly or arrogant, inattentive or lost in dreams, be they smiling still or plunged in tears; for they know the things that we do not know, and have a lamp that we have lost. Their abiding-place is at the foot itself of the Inevitable, whose well-worn paths are visible to them more clearly than to us. And thence it is that their strange intuitions have come to them, their gravity at which we wonder; and we feel that, even in their most trifling actions, they are conscious of being upheld by the strong, unerring hands of the gods. I said before that they drew us nearer to the gates of our being: verily might we believe, when we are with them, that that primeval gate is opening, amidst the bewildering whisper that doubtless waited on the birth of things, then when speech was yet hushed, for fear lest command or forbidding should issue forth, unheard....

She will never cross the threshold of that gate; and she awaits us within, where are the fountain-heads. And when we come and knock from without, and she opens to our bidding, her hand will still keep hold of latch and key. She will look, for one instant, at the man who has been sent to her, and in that brief moment she has learned all that had to be learned, and the years to come have trembled to the end of time.... Who shall tell us of what consists the first look of love, 'that magic wand made of a ray of broken light,' the ray that has issued forth from the eternal home of our being, that has transformed two souls, and given them twenty centuries of youth? The door may open again, or close; pay no heed, nor make further effort, for all is decided. She knows. She will no longer concern herself with the things you do, or say, or even think; and if she notice them, it will be but with a smile, and unconsciously will she fling from her all that does not help to confirm the certitudes of that first glance. And if you think you have deceived her, and that her impression is wrong, be sure that it is she who is right, and you yourself who are mistaken; for you are more truly that which you are in her eyes than that which in your soul you believe yourself to be, and this even though she may forever misinterpret the meaning of a gesture, a smile or a tear....

Hidden treasures that have not even a name!... I would that all those who have suffered at women's hands, and found them evil, would loudly proclaim it, and give us their reasons; and if those reasons be well founded we shall be indeed surprised, and shall have advanced far forward in the mystery. For women are indeed the veiled sisters of all the great things we do not see. They are indeed nearest of kin to the infinite that is about us, and they alone can still smile at it with the intimate grace of the child, to whom its father inspires no fear. It is they who preserve here below the pure fragrance of our soul, like some jewel from Heaven, which none know how to use; and were they to depart, the spirit would reign in solitude in a desert. Theirs are still the divine emotions of the first days; and the sources of their being lie, deeper far than ours, in all that was illimitable. Those who complain of them know not the heights whereon the true kisses are to be found, and verily do I pity them. And yet, how insignificant do women seem when we look at them as we pass by! We see them moving about in their little homes; this one is bending forward, down there another is sobbing, a third sings and the last sews; and there is not one of us who understands.... We visit them, as one visits pleasant things; we approach them with caution and suspicion, and it is scarcely possible for the soul to enter. We question them, mistrustfully—they, who know already, answer naught, and we go away, shrugging our shoulders, convinced that they do not understand.... 'But what need for them to understand,' answers the poet, who is always right, 'what need for them to understand, those thrice happy ones who have chosen the better part, and who, even as a pure flame of love in this earth of ours, token of the celestial fire that irradiates all things, shine forth only from the pinnacles of temples and the mastheads of ships that wander? Some of Nature's strangest secrets are often revealed, at sacred moments, to these maidens who love, and ingenuously and unconsciously will they declare them. The sage follows in their footsteps to gather up the jewels, that in their innocence and joy they scatter along the path. The poet, who feels what they feel, offers homage to their love, and tries, in his songs, to transplant that love, that is the germ of the age of gold, to other times and other countries.' For what has been said of the mystics applies above all to women, since it is they who have preserved the sense of the mystic in our earth to this day....

THE TRAGICAL IN DAILY LIFE

THERE is a tragic element in the life of every day that is far more real, far more penetrating, far more akin to the true self that is in us than the tragedy that lies in great adventure. But, readily as we all may feel this, to prove it is by no means easy, inasmuch as this essential tragic element comprises more than that which is merely material or merely psychological. It goes beyond the determined struggle of man against man, and desire against desire: it goes beyond the eternal conflict of duty and passion. Its province is rather to reveal to us how truly wonderful is the mere act of living, and to throw light upon the existence of the soul, self-contained in the midst of ever-restless immensities; to hush the discourse of reason and sentiment, so that above the tumult may be heard the solemn, uninterrupted whisperings of man and his destiny. It is its province to point out to us the uncertain, dolorous footsteps of the being, as he approaches, or wanders from, his truth, his beauty, or his God. And further, to show us, and make us understand, the countless other things therewith connected, of which tragic poets have but vouchsafed us passing glimpses. And here do we come to an essential point, for could not these things, of which we have had only passing glimpses, be placed in front of the others, and shown to us first of all? The mysterious chant of the Infinite, the ominous silence of the soul and of God, the murmur of Eternity on the horizon, the destiny or fatality that we are conscious of within us, though by what tokens none can tell—do not all these underlie King Lear, Macbeth, Hamlet? And would it not be possible, by some interchanging of the rôles, to bring them nearer to us, and send the actors farther off? Is it beyond the mark to say that the true tragic element, normal, deep-rooted, and universal, that the true tragic element of life only begins at the moment when so-called adventures, sorrows, and dangers have disappeared? Is the arm of happiness not longer than that of sorrow, and do not certain of its attributes draw nearer to the soul? Must we indeed roar like the Atrides, before the Eternal God will reveal Himself in our life? and is He never by our side at times when the air is calm, and the lamp burns on, unflickering? When we think of it, is it not the tranquillity that is terrible, the tranquillity watched by the stars? and is it in tumult or in silence that the spirit of life quickens within us? Is it not when we are told, at the end of the story, 'They were happy,' that the great disquiet should intrude itself? What is taking place while they are happy? Are there not elements of deeper gravity and stability in happiness, in a single moment of repose, than in the whirlwind of passion? Is it not then that we at last behold the march of time—ay, and of many another on-stealing besides, more secret still—is it not then that the hours rush forward? Are not deeper chords set vibrating by all these things than by the dagger-stroke of conventional drama? Is it not at the very moment when a man believes himself secure from bodily death that the strange and silent tragedy of the being and the immensities does indeed raise its curtain on the stage? Is it while I flee before a naked sword that my existence touches its most interesting point? Is life always at its sublimest in a kiss? Are there not other moments, when one hears purer voices that do not fade away so soon? Does the soul only flower on nights of storm? Hitherto, doubtless, this belief has prevailed. It is only the life of violence, the life of bygone days, that is perceived by nearly all our tragic writers; and truly may one say that anachronism dominates the stage, and that dramatic art dates back as many years as the art of sculpture. Far different is it with the other arts—with painting and music, for instance—for these have learned to select and reproduce those obscurer phases of daily life that are not the less deep-rooted and amazing. They know that all that life has lost, as regards mere superficial ornament, has been more than counterbalanced by the depth, the intimate meaning and the spiritual gravity it has acquired. The true artist no longer chooses Marius triumphing over the Cimbrians, or the assassination of the Duke of Guise, as fit subjects for his art; for he is well aware that the psychology of victory or murder is but elementary and exceptional, and that the solemn voice of men and things, the voice that issues forth so timidly and hesitatingly, cannot be heard amidst the idle uproar of acts of violence. And therefore will he place on his canvas a house lost in the heart of the country, an open door at the end of a passage, a face or hands at rest, and by these simple images will he add to our consciousness of life, which is a possession that it is no longer possible to lose.

But to the tragic author, as to the mediocre painter who still lingers over historical pictures, it is only the violence of the anecdote that appeals, and in his representation thereof does the entire interest of his work consist. And he imagines, forsooth, that we shall delight in witnessing the very same acts that brought joy to the hearts of the barbarians, with whom murder, outrage and treachery were matters of daily occurrence. Whereas it is far away from bloodshed, battle-cry and sword-thrust that the lives of most of us flow on, and men's tears are silent to-day, and invisible, and almost spiritual....

Indeed, when I go to a theatre, I feel as though I were spending a few hours with my ancestors, who conceived life as something that was primitive, arid and brutal; but this conception of theirs scarcely even lingers in my memory, and surely it is not one that I can share. I am shown a deceived husband killing his wife, a woman poisoning her lover, a son avenging his father, a father slaughtering his children, children putting their father to death, murdered kings, ravished virgins, imprisoned citizens—in a word, all the sublimity of tradition, but alas, how superficial and material! Blood, surface-tears and death! What can I learn from creatures who have but one fixed idea, and who have no time to live, for that there is a rival, or a mistress, whom it behoves them to put to death?

I had hoped to be shown some act of life, traced back to its sources and to its mystery by connecting links, that my daily occupations afford me neither power nor occasion to study. I had gone thither hoping that the beauty, the grandeur and the earnestness of my humble day by day existence would, for one instant, be revealed to me, that I would be shown the I know not what presence, power or God that is ever with me in my room. I was yearning for one of the strange moments of a higher life that flit unperceived through my dreariest hours; whereas, almost invariably, all that I beheld was but a man who would tell me, at wearisome length, why he was jealous, why he poisoned, or why he killed.

I admire Othello, but he does not appear to me to live the august daily life of a Hamlet, who has the time to live, inasmuch as he does not act. Othello is admirably jealous. But is it not perhaps an ancient error to imagine that it is at the moments when this passion, or others of equal violence, possesses us, that we live our truest lives? I have grown to believe that an old man, seated in his armchair, waiting patiently, with his lamp beside him; giving unconscious ear to all the eternal laws that reign about his house, interpreting, without comprehending, the silence of doors and windows and the quivering voice of the light, submitting with bent head to the presence of his soul and his destiny—an old man, who conceives not that all the powers of this world, like so many heedful servants, are mingling and keeping vigil in his room, who suspects not that the very sun itself is supporting in space the little table against which he leans, or that every star in heaven and every fibre of the soul are directly concerned in the movement of an eyelid that closes, or a thought that springs to birth—I have grown to believe that he, motionless as he is, does yet live in reality a deeper, more human and more universal life than the lover who strangles his mistress, the captain who conquers in battle, or 'the husband who avenges his honour.'

I shall be told, perhaps, that a motionless life would be invisible, that therefore animation must be conferred upon it, and movement, and that such varied movement as would be acceptable is to be found only in the few passions of which use has hitherto been made. I do not know whether it be true that a static theatre is impossible. Indeed, to me it seems to exist already. Most of the tragedies of Æschylus are tragedies without movement. In both the 'Prometheus' and the 'Suppliants,' events are lacking; and the entire tragedy of the 'Chœphoræ'—surely the most terrible drama of antiquity— does but cling, nightmare-like, around the tomb of Agamemnon, till murder darts forth, as a lightning flash, from the accumulation of prayers, ever falling back upon themselves. Consider, from this point of view, a few more of the finest tragedies of the ancients: 'The Eumenides,' 'Antigone,' 'Electra,'

'Œdipus at Colonos.' 'They have admired,' said Racine in his preface to 'Berenice,' 'they have admired the "Ajax" of Sophocles, wherein there is nothing but Ajax killing himself with regret for the fury into which he fell after the arms of Achilles were denied him. They have admired "Philoctetes," whose entire subject is but the coming of Ulysses with intent to seize the arrows of Hercules. Even the "Œdipus," though full of recognitions, contains less subject-matter than the simplest tragedy of our days.'

What have we here but life that is almost motionless? In most cases, indeed, you will find that psychological action—infinitely loftier in itself than mere material action, and truly, one might think, well-nigh indispensable—that psychological action even has been suppressed, or at least vastly diminished, in a truly marvellous fashion, with the result that the interest centres solely and entirely in the individual, face to face with the universe. Here we are no longer with the barbarians, nor is man now fretting, himself in the midst of elementary passions, as though, forsooth, these were the only things worthy of note: he is at rest, and we have time to observe him. It is no longer a violent, exceptional moment of life that passes before our eyes—it is life itself. Thousands and thousands of laws there are, mightier and more venerable than those of passion; but, in common with all that is endowed with resistless force, these laws are silent, and discreet, and slow-moving; and hence it is only in the twilight that they can be seen and heard, in the meditation that comes to us at the tranquil moments of life.

When Ulysses and Neoptolemus come to Philoctetes and demand of him the arms of Hercules, their action is in itself as simple and ordinary as that of a man of our day who goes into a house to visit an invalid, of a traveller who knocks at the door of an inn, or of a mother who, by the fireside, awaits the return of her child. Sophocles indicates the character of his heroes by means of the lightest and quickest of touches. But it may safely be said that the chief interest of the tragedy does not lie in the struggle we witness between cunning and loyalty, between love of country, rancour, and headstrong pride. There is more beyond: for it is man's loftier existence that is laid bare to us. The poet adds to ordinary life something, I know not what, which is the poet's secret: and there comes to us a sudden revelation of life in its stupendous grandeur, in its submissiveness to the unknown powers, in its endless affinities, in its awe-inspiring misery. Let but the chemist pour a few mysterious drops into a vessel that seems to contain the purest water, and at once masses of crystals will rise to the surface, thus revealing to us all that lay in abeyance there where nothing was visible before to our incomplete eyes. And even thus is it in 'Philoctetes'; the primitive psychology of the three leading characters would seem to be merely the sides of the vessel containing the clear water; and this itself is our ordinary life, into which the poet is about to let fall the revelation-bearing drops of his genius....

Indeed, it is not in the actions but in the words that are found the beauty and greatness of tragedies that are truly beautiful and great; and this not solely in the words that accompany and explain the action, for there must perforce be another dialogue besides the one which is superficially necessary. And indeed the only words that count in the play are those that at first seemed useless, for it is therein that the essence lies. Side by side with the necessary dialogue will you almost always find another dialogue that seems superfluous; but examine it carefully, and it will be borne home to you that this is the only one that the soul can listen to profoundly, for here alone is it the soul that is being addressed. You will see, too, that it is the quality and the scope of this unnecessary dialogue that determine the quality and the immeasurable range of the work. Certain it is that, in the ordinary drama, the indispensable dialogue by no means corresponds to reality; and it is just those words that are spoken by the side of the rigid, apparent truth, that constitute the mysterious beauty of the most beautiful tragedies, inasmuch as these are words that conform to a deeper truth, and one that lies incomparably nearer to the invisible soul by which the poem is upheld. One may even affirm that a poem draws the nearer to beauty and loftier truth in the measure that it eliminates words that merely explain the action, and substitutes for them others that reveal, not the so-called 'soul-state,' but I know not what intangible and unceasing striving of the soul towards its own beauty and truth. And so much the nearer, also, does it draw to the true life. To every man does it happen, in his work-a-day existence, that some situation of deep seriousness has to be unravelled by means of words. Reflect for an instant. At moments such as those—nay, at the most commonplace of times—is it the thing you say or the reply you receive that has the most value? Are not other forces, other words one cannot hear, brought into being, and do not these determine the event? What I say often counts for so little; but my presence, the attitude of my soul, my future and my past, that which will take birth in me and that which is dead, a secret thought, the stars that approve, my destiny, the thousands of mysteries which surround me and float about yourself—all this it is that speaks to you at that tragic moment, all this it is that brings to me your answer. There is all this beneath every one of my words, and each one of yours; it is this, above all, that we see, it a this, above all, that we hear, ourselves notwithstanding. If you have come, you, the 'outraged husband,' the 'deceived lover,' the 'forsaken wife,' intending to kill me, your arm will not be stayed by my most moving entreaty; but it may be that there will come towards you, at that moment, one of these unexpected forces; and my soul, knowing of their vigil near to me, may whisper a secret word whereby, haply, you shall be disarmed. These are the spheres wherein adventures come to issue, this is the dialogue whose echo should be heard. And it is this echo that one does hear—extremely attenuated and variable, it is true—in some of the great works mentioned above. But might we not try to draw nearer to the spheres where it is 'in reality' that everything comes to pass?

It would seem as though the endeavour were being made. Some time ago, when dealing with 'The Master Builder,' which is the one of Ibsen's dramas wherein this dialogue of the 'second degree' attains the deepest tragedy, I endeavoured, unskilfully enough, to fix its secrets. For indeed they are kindred handmarks traced on the same wall by the same sightless being, groping for the same light. 'What is it,' I asked, 'what is it that, in the "Master Builder," the poet has added to life, thereby making it appear so strange, so profound and so disquieting beneath its trivial surface?' The discovery is not easy, and the old master hides from us more than one secret. It would even seem as though what he has wished to say were but little by the side of what he has been compelled to say. He has freed certain powers of the soul that have never yet been free, and it may well be that these have held him in thrall. 'Look you, Hilda,' exclaims Solness, 'look you! There is sorcery in you, too, as there is in me. It is this sorcery that imposes action on the powers of the beyond. And we *have* to yield to it. Whether we want to or not, we *must*.'

There is sorcery in them, as in us all. Hilda and Solness are, I believe, the first characters in drama who feel, for an instant, that they are living in the atmosphere of the soul; and the discovery of this essential life that exists in them, beyond the life of every day, comes fraught with terror. Hilda and Solness are two souls to whom a flash has revealed their situation in the true life. Diverse ways there are by which knowledge of our fellows may come to us. Two or three men, perhaps, are seen by me almost daily. For a long time it is merely by their gestures that I distinguish them, by their habits, be these of mind or body, by the manner in which they feel, act or think. But, in the course of every friendship of some duration, there comes to us a mysterious moment when we seem to perceive the exact relationship of our friend to the unknown that surrounds him, when we discover the attitude destiny has assumed towards him. And it is from this moment that he truly belongs to us. We have seen, once and for all, the treatment held in store for him by events. We know that however such a one may seclude himself in the recesses of his dwelling, in dread lest his slightest movement stir up that which lies in the great reservoirs of the future, his forethought will avail him nothing, and the innumerable events that destiny holds in reserve will discover him wherever he hide, and will knock one after another at his door. And even so do we know that this other will sally forth in vain in pursuit of adventure. He will ever return empty-handed. No sooner are our eyes thus opened than unerring knowledge would seem to spring to life, self-created, within our soul; and we know with absolute conviction that the event that seems to be impending over the head of a certain man will nevertheless most assuredly not reach him.

From this moment a special part of the soul reigns over the friendship of even the most unintelligent, the obscurest of men. Life has become, as it were, transposed. And when it happens that we meet one of the men who are thus known to us, though we do but speak of the snow that is falling or the women that pass by, something there is in each of us which nods to the other, which examines and asks its questions without our knowledge, which interests itself in contingencies and hints at events that it is impossible for us to understand....

Thus do I conceive it to be with Hilda and Solness; it is thus surely that they regard each other. Their conversation resembles nothing that we have ever heard, inasmuch as the poet has endeavoured to blend in one expression both the inner and the outer dialogue. A new, indescribable power dominates this somnambulistic drama. All that is said therein at once hides and reveals the sources of an unknown life. And if we are bewildered at times, let us not forget that our soul often appears to our feeble eyes to be but the maddest of forces, and that there are in man many regions more fertile, more profound and more interesting than those of his reason or his intelligence....

THE STAR

WELL might it be said that, from century to century, a tragic poet 'has wandered through the labyrinths of destiny with the torch of poesy in his hand.' For in this way has each one, according to the forces of his hour, fixed the souls of the annals of man, and it is divine history that has thus been composed. It is in the poets alone that we can follow the countless variations of the great unchanging power; and to follow them is indeed interesting, for at the root of the idea that they have formed of this power is to be found, perhaps, the purest essence of a nation's soul. It is a power that has never entirely ceased to be, yet moments there are when it scarcely seems to stir; and at such moments one feels that life is neither very active nor very profound. Once only has it been the object of undivided worship; then was it, even for the gods, an awe-inspiring mystery. And there is a thing that is passing strange—it was the very period when the featureless divinity seemed most terrible and most incomprehensible that was the most beautiful period of mankind, and the people to whom destiny wore the most formidable aspect were the happiest people of all.

It would seem that a secret force must underlie this idea, or that the idea is itself the manifestation of a force. Does man develop in the measure that he recognises the greatness of the unknown that sways him, or is it the unknown that develops in proportion to the man? To-day the idea of destiny would seem to be again awakening, and to go forth in search of it were perhaps no unprofitable quest. But where shall it be found? To go in search of destiny— what is this but to seek all the sorrows of man? There is no destiny of joy, no star that bodes of happiness. The star that is so called is only a star of forbearance. Yet is it well that we should sally forth at times in search of our sorrows, so that we may learn to know them and admire them; and this even though the great shapeless mass of destiny be not encountered at the end.

Seeking our sorrows, we shall be the most effectively seeking ourselves, for truly may it be said that the value of ourselves is but the value of our melancholy and our disquiet. As we progress, so do they become deeper, nobler and more beautiful; and Marcus Aurelius is to be admired above all men, because, better than all men, has he understood how much there is of the soul in the meek resigned smile it must wear, at the depths of us. Thus is it, too, with the sorrows of humanity. They follow a road which resembles the road of our own sorrows; but it is longer, and surer, and must lead to fatherlands that the last comers alone shall know. This road also has physical sorrow for its starting-point; it has only just rounded the fear of the gods, and to-day it halts by a new abyss, whose depths the very best of us have not yet sounded.

Each century holds another sorrow dear, for each century discerns another destiny. Certain it is that we no longer interest ourselves, as was formerly the case, in the catastrophes of passion; and the quality of the sorrow revealed in the most tragic masterpieces of the past is inferior to the quality of the sorrows of to-day. It is only indirectly that these tragedies affect us now; only by means of that which is brought to bear on the simple accidents of love or hatred they reproduce, by the reflection and new nobility of sentiment that the pain of living has created within us.

There are moments when it would seem as though we were on the threshold of a new pessimism, mysterious and, perhaps, very pure. The most redoubtable sages, Schopenhauer, Carlyle, the Russians, the Scandinavians, and the good optimist Emerson, too (for than a wilful optimist there is nothing more discouraging), all these have passed our melancholy by, unexplained. We feel that, underlying all the reasons they have essayed to give us, there are many other profounder reasons, whose discovery has been beyond them. The sadness of man which seemed beautiful even to them, is still susceptible of infinite ennobling, until at last a creature of genius shall have uttered the final word of the sorrow that shall, perhaps, wholly purify....

In the meanwhile, we are in the hands of strange powers, whose intentions we are on the eve of divining. At the time of the great tragic writers of the new era, at the time of Shakespeare, Racine, and their successors, the belief prevailed that all misfortunes came from the various passions of the heart. Catastrophes did not hover between two worlds: they came hence to go thither, and their point of departure was known. Man was always the master. Much less was this the case at the time of the Greeks, for then did fatality reign on the heights; but it was inaccessible, and none dared interrogate it. To-day it is fatality that we challenge, and this is perhaps the distinguishing note of the new theatre. It is no longer the effects of disaster that arrest our attention; it is disaster itself, and we are eager to know its essence and its laws. It was the *nature* of disaster with which the earliest tragic writers were, all unconsciously, preoccupied, and this it was that, though they knew it not, threw a solemn shadow round the hard and violent gestures of external death; and it is this, too, that has become the rallying-point of the most recent dramas, the centre of light with strange flames gleaming, about which revolve the souls of women and of men. And a step has been taken towards the mystery so that life's terrors may be looked in the face.

It would be interesting to discover from what point of view our latest tragic writers appear to regard the disaster that forms the basis of all dramatic poems. They see it from a nearer point of vision than the Greeks, and they have penetrated deeper into the fertile darknesses of its inner circle. The divinity is perhaps the same; they know nothing of it, yet do they study it more closely. Whence does it come, whither does it go, why does it descend upon us? These were problems to which the Greeks barely gave a thought. Is it written within us, or is it born at the same time as ourselves? Does it of its own accord start forward to meet us, or is it summoned by conniving voices that we cherish at the depths of us? If we could but follow, from the heights of another world, the ways of the man over whom a great sorrow is impending! And what man is there that does not laboriously, though all unconsciously, himself fashion the sorrow that is to be the pivot of his life!

The Scotch peasants have a word that might be applied to every existence. In their legends they give the name of 'Fey' to the frame of mind of a man who, notwithstanding all his efforts, notwithstanding all help and advice, is forced by some irresistible impulse, towards an inevitable catastrophe. It is thus that James I., the James of Catherine Douglas, was 'fey' when he went, notwithstanding the terrible omens of earth, heaven and hell, to spend the Christmas holidays in the gloomy castle of Perth, where his assassin, the traitor Robert Graeme, lay in wait for him. Which of us, recalling the circumstances of the most decisive misfortune of his life, but has felt himself similarly possessed? Be it well understood that I speak here only of active misfortunes, of those that might have been prevented: for there are passive misfortunes (such as the death of a person we adore) which simply come towards us, and cannot be influenced by any movement of ours. Bethink you of the fatal day of your life. Have we not all been forewarned; and though it may seem to us now that destiny might have been changed by a step we did not take, a door we did not open, a hand we did not raise, which of us but has struggled vainly on the topmost walls of the abyss, struggled without vigour and without hope, against a force that was invisible and apparently without power?

The breath of air stirred by the door I opened, one evening, was for ever to extinguish my happiness, as it would have extinguished a flickering lamp; and now, when I think of it, I cannot tell myself that I did not know.... And yet, it was nothing important that had taken me to the threshold. I could have gone away, shrugging my shoulders: there was no human reason that could force me to knock on the panel. No human reason, nothing but destiny....

*

Herein there is still some resemblance to the fatality of Œdipus, and yet it is already different. One might say that it is this same fatality seen *ab intra*. Mysterious powers hold sway within us, and these would seem to be in league with adventures. We all cherish enemies within our soul. They know what they do and what they force us to do, and when they lead us to the event, they let fall half-uttered words of warning—too few to stop us on the road—but sufficient to make us regret, when it is too late, that we did not listen more attentively to their wavering, ironical advice. What object can they have, these powers that seek our destruction as though they were self-existing and did not perish with us, seeing that it is in us only that they have life? What is it that sets in motion all the confederates of the universe, who fatten on our blood?

The man for whom the hour of misfortune has sounded is caught up by an invisible whirlwind, and for years back have these powers been combining the innumerable incidents that must bring him to the necessary moment, to the exact spot where tears lie in wait for him. Remember all your efforts, all your presentiments, all the unavailing offers of help. Remember, too, the kindly circumstances that pitied you, and tried to bar your passage, but you thrust them aside like so many importunate beggars. And yet were they humble, timid sisters, who desired but to save you, and they went away without saying a word, too weak and too helpless to struggle against decided things—where decided it is known to God alone....

Scarcely has the disaster befallen us than we have the strange sensation of having obeyed an eternal law; and, in the midst of the greatest sorrow, there is I know not what mysterious comfort that rewards us for our obedience. Never do we belong more completely to ourselves than on the morrow of an irreparable catastrophe. It seems, then, as though we had found ourselves again, as though we had won back a part of ourselves that was necessary and unknown. A curious calm steals over us. For days past, almost without our knowledge, notwithstanding that we were able to smile at faces and flowers, the rebel forces of our soul had been waging terrible battle on the borders of the abyss, and now that we are at the depths of it, all breathes freely.

Even thus, without respite, do these rebel forces struggle in the soul of every one of us; and there are times when we may see the shadow of these combats wherein our soul may not intervene, but we pay no heed, for to all save the unimportant do we shut our eyes. At a time when my friends are about me it may happen that, in the midst of talk and shouts of laughter, there shall suddenly steal over the face of one of them something that is not of this world. A motiveless silence shall instantly prevail, and for a second's space all shall be unconsciously looking forth with the eyes of the soul. Whereupon, the words and smiles, that had disappeared like frightened frogs in a lake, will again mount to the surface, more violent than before. But the invisible, here as everywhere, has gathered its tribute. Something has understood that a fight was over, that a star was rising or falling and that a destiny had just been decided....

Perhaps it had been decided before; and who knows whether the struggle be not a mere simulacrum? If I push open to-day the door of the house wherein I am to meet the first smiles of a sorrow that shall know no end, I do these things for a longer time than one imagines. Of what avail to cultivate an ego on which we have so little influence? It is our star which it behoves us to watch. It is good or bad, pallid or puissant, and not by all the might of the sea can it be changed. Some there are who may confidently play with their star as one might play with a glass ball. They may throw it and hazard it where they list; faithfully will it ever return to their hands. They know full well that it cannot be broken. But there are many others who dare not even raise their eyes towards their star, without it detach itself from the firmament and fall in dust at their feet....

But it is dangerous to speak of the star, dangerous even to think of it; for it is often the sign that it is on the point of extinction....

We find ourselves here in the abysses of night, where we await what has to be. There is no longer question of free will, which we have left thousands of leagues below: we are in a region where the will itself is but destiny's ripest fruit. We must not complain; something is already known to us, and we have discovered a few of the ways of fortune. We lie in wait like the birdcatcher studying the habits of migratory birds, and when an event is signalled on the horizon we know full well that it will not remain there alone, but that its brothers will flock in troops to the same spot. Vaguely have we learned that there are certain thoughts, certain souls, that attract events; that some beings there are who divert events in their flight, as there are others who cause them to congregate from the four quarters of the globe.

Above all do we know that certain ideas are fraught with extreme danger; that do we but for an instant deem ourselves in safety, this alone suffices to draw down the thunderbolt; we know that happiness creates a void, into which tears will speedily be hurled. After a time, too, we learn something of the preferences of events. It is soon borne home to us that if we take a few steps along the path of life by the side of this one of our brothers, the ways of fortune will no longer be the same, whereas, with this other, our existence will encounter unvarying events, coming in regular order. We feel that some beings there are who protect in the unknown, others who drag us into danger there; we feel that there are some who awaken the future, others who lull it into slumber. We suspect, further, that things at their birth are but feeble, that they draw their force from within us, and that, in every adventure, there is a brief moment when our instinct warns us that we are still the lords of destiny. In fine, there are some who dare assert that we can learn to be happy, that, as we become better, so do we meet men of loftier mind; that a man who is good attracts, with irresistible force, events as good as he, and that, in a beautiful soul, the saddest fortune is transformed into beauty....

Indeed, is it not within the knowledge of us all that goodness beckons to goodness, and that those for whom we devote ourselves are always the same; that they are always the same, those whom we betray? When the same sorrow knocks at two adjoining doors, at the houses of the just and the unjust, will its method of action be identical in both? If you are pure, will not your misfortunes be pure? To have known how to change the past into a few saddened smiles—is this not to master the future? And does it not seem that, even in the inevitable, there is something we can keep back? Do not great hazards lie dormant that a too sudden movement of ours may awaken on the horizon; and would this misfortune have befallen you to-day, but for the thoughts that this morning kept too noisy festival in your soul? Is this all that our wisdom has been able to glean in the darkness? Who would dare affirm that in these regions there be more substantial truths? In the meanwhile, let us learn how to smile, let us learn how to weep, in the silence of humblest kindliness. Slowly there rises above these things the shrouded face of the destiny of to-day. Of the veil that formerly covered it, a minute corner has been lifted, and there, where the veil is not, do we recognise, to our disquiet, on the one side, *the power of those who live not yet*, on the other, *the power of the dead*. The mystery has again been shifted further from us—that is all. We have enlarged the icy hand of destiny; and we find that, in its shadow, the hands of our ancestors are clasped by the hands of our sons yet unborn. One act there was that we deemed the sanctuary of all our rights, and love remained the supreme refuge of all those on whom the chains of life weighed too heavily. Here, at least, in the isolation of this secret temple, we told ourselves that no one entered with us. Here, for an instant, we could breathe; here, at last, it was our soul that reigned, and free was its choice in that which was the centre of liberty itself! But now we are told that it is not for our own sake that we love. We are told that in the very temple of love we do but obey the unvarying orders of an invisible throng. We are told that a thousand centuries divide us from ourselves when we choose the woman we love, and that the first kiss of the betrothed is but the seal that thousands of hands, craving for birth, impress upon the lips of the mother they desire. And, further, we know that the dead do not die. We know now that it is not in our churches that they are to be found, but in the houses, the habits, of us all. That there is not a gesture, a thought, a sin, a tear, an atom of acquired consciousness that is lost in the depths of the earth; and that at the most insignificant of our acts our ancestors arise, not in their tombs where they move not, but in ourselves, where they always live....

Thus are we led by past and future. And the present, which is the substance of us, sinks to the bottom of the sea, like some tiny island at which two irreconcilable oceans have been unceasingly gnawing. Heredity, will, destiny, all mingle noisily in our soul; but, notwithstanding everything, far above everything, it is the silent star that reigns. No matter with what temporary labels we may bedeck the monstrous vases that contain the invisible, words can tell us scarcely anything of that which should be told. Heredity, nay destiny itself, what are these but a ray of this star, a ray that is lost in the mysterious night? And all that is might well be more mysterious still. 'We give the name of destiny to all that limits us,' says one of the great sages of our time: wherefore it behoves us to be grateful to all those who tremblingly grope their way the side of the frontier. 'If we are brutal and barbarous,' he goes on, 'fatality takes a form that is brutal and barbarous. As refinement comes to us, so do our mishaps become refined. If we rise to spiritual culture, antagonism takes unto itself a spiritual form.' It is perhaps true that even as our soul soars aloft, so does it purify destiny, although it is also true that we are menaced by the self-same sorrows that menace the savages. But we have other sorrows of which they have no suspicion; and the spirit, as it rises, does but discover still more, at every horizon. 'We give the name of destiny to all that limits us.' Let us do our utmost that destiny become not too circumscribed. It is good to enlarge one's sorrows, since thus does enlargement come to our consciousness, and there, there alone do we truly feel that we live. And it is also the only means of fulfilling our supreme duty towards other worlds; since it is probably on us alone that it is incumbent to augment the consciousness of the earth.

THE INVISIBLE GOODNESS

IT is a thing, said to me one evening the sage I had chanced to meet by the sea shore, whereon the waves were breaking almost noiselessly—it is a thing that we scarcely notice, that none seem to take into account, and yet do I conceive it to be one of the forces that safeguard mankind. In a thousand diverse ways do the gods from whom we spring reveal themselves within us, but it may well be that this unnoticed secret goodness, to which sufficiently direct allusion has never yet been made, is the purest token of their eternal life. Whence it comes we know not. It is there in its simplicity, smiling on the threshold of our soul; and those in whom its smiles lie deepest, or shine forth most frequently, may make us suffer day and night and they will, yet shall it be beyond our power to cease to love them....

It is not of this world, and still are there few agitations of ours in which it takes not part. It cares not to reveal itself even in look or tear. Nay, it seeks concealment, for reasons one cannot divine. It is as though it were afraid to make use of its power. It knows that its most involuntary movement will cause immortal things to spring to life about it; and we are miserly with immortal things. Why are we so fearful lest we exhaust the heaven within us? We dare not act upon the whisper of the God who inspires us. We are afraid of everything that cannot be explained by word or gesture: and we shut our eyes to all that we do, ourselves notwithstanding, in the empire where explanations are vain! Whence comes the timidity of the divine in man? For truly might it be said that the nearer a movement of our soul approaches the divine, so much the more scrupulously do we conceal it from the eyes of our brethren. Can it be that man is nothing but a frightened god? Or has the command been laid upon us that the superior powers must not be betrayed? Upon all that does not form part of this too visible world there rests the tender meekness of the little ailing girl, for whom her mother will not send when strangers come to the house. And therefore it is that this secret goodness of ours has never yet passed through the silent portals of our soul. It lives within us like a prisoner forbidden to approach the barred window of her cell. But indeed, what matter though it do not approach? Enough that it be there. Hide as it may, let it but raise its head, move a link of its chain or open its hand, and the prison is illumined, the pressure of radiance from within bursts open the iron barrier, and then, suddenly, there yawns a gulf between words and beings, a gulf peopled with agitated angels: silence falls over all: the eyes turn away for a moment and two souls embrace tearfully on the threshold....

It is not a thing that comes from this earth of ours, and all descriptions can be of no avail. They who would understand must have, in themselves too, *the same point of sensibility*. If you have never in your life felt the power of *your invisible goodness*, go no further; it would be useless. But are there really any who have not felt this power, and have the worst of us never been invisibly good? I know not: of so many in this world does the aim seem to be the discouragement of the divine in their soul. And yet there needs but one instant of respite for the divine to spring up again, and even the wickedest are not incessantly on their guard; and hence doubtless has it arisen that so many of the wicked are good, unseen of all, whereas divers saints and sages are not invisibly good....

More than once have I been the cause of suffering, he went on, even as each being is the cause of suffering about him. I have caused suffering because we are in a world where all is held together by invisible threads, in a world where none are alone, and where the gentlest gesture of love or kindliness may so often wound the innocence by our side!—I have caused suffering, too, because there are times when the best and tenderest are impelled to seek I know not what part of themselves in the grief of others. For, indeed, there are seeds that only spring up in our soul beneath the rain of tears shed because of us, and none the less do these seeds produce good flowers and salutary fruit. What would you? It is no law of our making, and I know not whether I would dare to love the man who had made no one weep. Frequently, indeed, will the greatest suffering be caused by those whose love is greatest, for a strange timid, tender cruelty is most often the anxious sister of love. On all sides does love search for the proofs of love, and the first proofs—who is not prone to discover them in the tears of the beloved?

Even death could not suffice to reassure the lover who dared to give ear to the unreasoning claims of love; for to the intimate cruelty of love, the instant of death seems too brief; over beyond death there is yet room for a sea of doubts, and even in those who die together may disquiet still linger as they die. Long, slowly falling tears are needed here. Grief is love's first food, and every love that has not been fed on a little pure suffering must die like the babe that one had tried to nourish on the nourishment of a man. Will the love inspired by the woman who always brought the smile to your lips be quite the same as the love you feel for her who at times called forth your tears? Alas! needs must love weep, and often indeed is it at the very moment when the sobs burst forth that love's chains are forged and tempered for life....

Thus, he continued, I have caused suffering because I loved, and also have I caused suffering because I did not love—but how great was the difference in the two cases! In the one the slowly dropping tears of well-tried love seemed already to know, at the depths of them, that they were bedewing all that was ineffable in our united souls; in the other the poor tears knew that they were falling in solitude on a desert. But it is at those very moments when the soul is all ear—or, haply, all soul—that I have recognised the might of an invisible goodness that could offer to the wretched tears of an expiring love the divine illusions of a love on the eve of birth. Has there never come to you one of those sorrowful evenings when dejection lay heavy upon your unsmiling kisses, and it at length dawned upon your soul that it had been mistaken? With direst difficulty did your words ring forth in the cold air of the separation that was to be final; you were about to part for ever, and your almost lifeless hands were outstretched for the farewell of a departure that should know no return, when suddenly your soul made an imperceptible movement within itself. On that instant did the soul by the side of you awake on the summits of its being; something sprang to life in regions loftier far than the love of jaded lovers; and for all that the bodies might shrink asunder, henceforth would the souls never forget that for an instant they had beheld each other high above mountains they had never seen, and that for a second's space they had been good with a goodness they had never known until that day....

What can this be, this mysterious movement that I speak of here in connection with love only, but which may well take place in the smallest events of life? Is it I know not what sacrifice or inner embrace, is it the profoundest desire to be soul for a soul, or the consciousness, ever quickening within us, of the presence of a life that is invisible, but equal to our own? Is it all that is admirable and sorrowful in the mere act of living that, at such moments, floods our being—is it the aspect of life, one and indivisible? I know not; but in truth it is then that we feel that there lurks, somewhere, an unknown force; it is then that we feel that we are the treasures of an unknown God who loves all, that not a gesture of this God may pass unperceived, and that we are at length in the region of things that do not betray themselves....

Certain it is that, from the day of our birth to the day of our death, we never emerge from this clearly defined region, but wander in God like helpless sleepwalkers, or like the blind who despairingly seek the very temple in which they do indeed befind themselves. We are there in life, man against man, soul against soul, and day and night are spent under arms. We never see each other, we never touch each other. We see nothing but bucklers and helmets, we touch nothing but iron and brass. But let a tiny circumstance, come from the simpleness of the sky, for one instant only cause the weapons to fall, are there not always tears beneath the helmet, childlike smiles behind the buckler, and is not another verity revealed?

He thought for a moment, then went on, more sadly: A woman—as I believe I told you just now—a woman to whom I had caused suffering against my will—for the most careful of us scatter suffering around them without their knowledge—a woman to whom I had caused suffering against my will, revealed to me one evening the sovereign power of this invisible good. To be good we must needs have suffered; but perhaps it is necessary to have caused suffering before we can become better. This was brought home to me that evening. I felt that I had arrived, alone, at that sad zone of kisses when it seems to us that we are visiting the hovels of the poor, while she, who had lingered on the road, was still smiling in the palace of the first days. Love, as men understand it, was dying between us like a child stricken with a disease come one knows not whence, a disease that has no pity. We said nothing. It would be impossible for me to recall what my thoughts were at that earnest moment. They were doubtless of no significance. I was probably thinking of the last face I had seen, of the quivering gleam of a lantern at a deserted street corner; and, nevertheless, *everything took place* in a light a thousand times purer, a thousand times higher, than had there intervened all the forces of pity and love which I command in my thoughts and my heart. We parted, and not a word was spoken, but at one and the same moment had we understood our inexpressible thought. We know now that another love had sprung to life, a love that demands not the words, the little attentions and smiles of ordinary love. We have never met again. Perhaps centuries will elapse before we ever do meet again.

'Much is to learn, much to forget,
Through worlds I shall traverse not a few'

before we shall again find ourselves *in the same movement of the soul* as on that evening: but we can well afford to wait....

And thus, ever since that day, have I greeted, in all places, even in the very bitterest of moments, the beneficent presence of this marvellous power. He who has but once clearly seen it, shall never again find it possible to turn away from its face. You will often behold it smiling in the last retreat of hatred, in the depths of the cruellest tears. And yet does it not reveal itself to the eyes of the body. Its nature changes from the moment that it manifests itself by means of an exterior act; and we are no longer in the truth according to the soul, but in a kind of falsehood as conceived by man. Goodness and love that are self-conscious have no influence on the soul, for they have departed from the kingdoms where they have their dwelling; but, do they only remain blind, they can soften Destiny itself. I have known more than one man who performed every act of kindness and mercy without touching a single soul; and I have known others, who seemed to live in falsehood and injustice, yet were no souls driven from them nor did any for an instant even believe that these men were not good. Nay, more, even those who do not know you, who are merely told of your acts of goodness and deeds of love— if you be not good according to the invisible goodness, these, even, will feel that something is lacking, and they will never be touched in the depths of their being. One might almost believe that there exists, somewhere, a place where all is weighed in the presence of the spirits, or perhaps, out yonder, the other side of the night, a reservoir of certitudes whither the silent herd of souls flock every morning to slake their thirst.

Perhaps we do not yet know what the word 'to love' means. There are within us lives in which we love unconsciously. To love thus means more than to have pity, to make inner sacrifices, to be anxious to help and give happiness; it is a thing that lies a thousand fathoms deeper, where our softest, swiftest, strongest words cannot reach it. At moments we might believe it to be a recollection, furtive but excessively keen, of the great primitive unity. There is in this love a force that nothing can resist. Which of us—an' he question himself the side of the light, from which our gaze is habitually averted—which of us but will find in himself the recollection of certain strange workings of this force? Which of us, when by the side of the most ordinary person perhaps, but has suddenly become conscious of the advent of something that none had summoned? Was it the soul, or perhaps life, that had turned within itself like a sleeper on the point of awakening? I know not; nor did you know, and no one spoke of it; but you did not separate from each other as though nothing had happened.

To love thus is to love according to the soul; and there is no soul that does not respond to this love. For the soul of man is a guest that has gone hungry these centuries back, and never has it to be summoned twice to the nuptial feast.

The souls of all our brethren are ever hovering about us, craving for a caress, and only waiting for the signal. But how many beings there are who all their life long have not dared make such a signal! It is the disaster of our entire existence that we live thus away from our soul, and stand in such dread of its slightest movement. Did we but allow it to smile frankly in its silence and its radiance, we should be already living an eternal life. We have only to think for an instant how much it succeeds in accomplishing during those rare moments when we knock off its chains—for it is our custom to enchain it as though it were distraught—what it does in love, for instance, for there we do permit it at times to approach the lattices of external life. And would it not be in accordance with the primal truth if all men were to feel that they were face to face with each other, even as the woman feels with the man she loves?

This invisible and divine goodness, of which I only speak here because of its being one of the surest and nearest signs of the unceasing activity of our soul, this invisible and divine goodness ennobles, in decisive fashion, all that it has unconsciously touched. Let him who has a grievance against his fellow, descend into himself and seek out whether he never has been good in the presence of that fellow. For myself, I have never met any one by whose side I have felt my invisible goodness bestir itself, without he has become, at that very instant, better than myself. Be good at the depths of you, and you will discover that those who surround you will be good even to the same depths. Nothing responds more infallibly to the secret cry of goodness than the secret cry of goodness that is near. While you are actively good in the invisible, all those who approach you will unconsciously do things that they could not do by the side of any other man. Therein lies a force that has no name; a spiritual rivalry that knows no resistance. It is as though this were the actual place where is the sensitive spot of our soul; for there are souls that seem to have forgotten their existence and to have renounced everything that enables the being to rise; but, once touched here, they all draw themselves erect; and in the divine plains of the secret goodness, the most humble of souls cannot endure defeat.

And yet it is possible that nothing is changing in the life one sees; but is it only that which matters, and is our existence indeed confined to actions we can take in our hand like stones on the high road? If you ask yourself, as we are told we should ask every evening, 'What of immortal have I done to-day?' Is it always on the material side that we can count, weigh and measure unerringly; is it there that you must begin your search? It is possible for you to cause extraordinary tears to flow; it is possible that you may fill a heart with unheard of certitudes, and give eternal life unto a soul, and no one shall know of it, nor shall you even know yourself. It may be that nothing is changing; it may be that were it put to the test all would crumble, and that this goodness we speak of would yield to the smallest fear. It matters not. Something divine has happened; and somewhere must our God have smiled. May it not be the supreme aim of life thus to bring to birth the inexplicable within ourselves; and do we know how much we add to ourselves when we awake something of the incomprehensible that slumbers in every corner? Here you have awakened love which will not fall asleep again. The soul that your soul has regarded, that has wept with you the holy tears of the solemn joy that none may behold, will bear you no resentment, not even in the midst of torture. It will not even feel the need of forgiving. So convinced is it of one knows not what, that nothing can henceforth dim or efface the smile that it wears within; for nothing can ever separate two souls which, for an instant, 'have been good together.'

THE DEEPER LIFE

IT is well that men should be reminded that the very humblest of them has the power to 'fashion, after a divine model that he chooses not, a great moral personality, composed in equal parts of himself and the ideal; and that if anything lives in fullest reality, of a surety it is that.'

Each man has to seek out his own special aptitude for a higher life in the midst of the humble and inevitable reality of daily existence. Than this there can be no nobler aim in life. It is only by the communications we have with the infinite that we are to be distinguished from each other. If the hero is greater than the wretch who marches by his side, it is because at a certain moment of his existence there has come to him a fuller consciousness of one of these communications. If it is true that creation does not stop at man and that we are surrounded by invisible beings who are superior to us, their superiority can only consist in that they have, with the infinite, communications whose nature we cannot even imagine.

It lies within our power to increase these communications. In the life of every man has there been a day when the heavens opened of their own accord, and it is almost always from that very instant that dates his true spiritual personality. It is doubtless at that instant that are formed the invisible, eternal features that we reveal, though we know it not, to angels and to souls. But with most men it is chance alone that has caused the heavens to open; and they have not chosen the face whereby the angels know them in the infinite, nor have they understood how to ennoble and purify its features—which do indeed but owe their being to an accidental joy or sadness, an accidental thought or fear.

Our veritable birth dates from the day when, for the first time, we feel at the deepest of us that there is something grave and unexpected in life. Some there are who realise suddenly that they are not alone under the sky. To others will it be brusquely revealed, while shedding a tear or giving a kiss, that 'the source of all that is good and holy from the universe up to God is hidden behind a night, full of too distant stars'; a third will see a divine hand stretched forth between his joy and his misfortune; and yet another will have understood that it is the dead who are in the right. One will have had pity, another will have admired or been afraid. Often does it need almost nothing, a word, a gesture, a little thing that is not even a thought. 'Before, I loved thee as a brother, John,' says one of Shakespeare's heroes, admiring the other's action, 'but now I do respect thee as my soul.' On that day it is probable that a being will have come into the world.

We can be born thus more than once; and each birth brings us a little nearer to our God. But most of us are content to wait till an event, charged with almost irresistible radiance, intrudes itself violently upon our darkness, and enlightens us, in our despite. We await I know not what happy coincidence, when it may so come about that the eyes of our soul shall be open at the very moment that something extraordinary takes place. But in everything that happens is there light; and the greatness of the greatest of men has but consisted in that they had trained their eyes to be open to every ray of this light. Is it indeed essential that your mother should breathe her last in your arms, that your children should perish in a shipwreck, and that you yourself should pass by the side of death, for you at length to understand that you have your being in an incomprehensible world where you shall be for ever, where an unseen God, who is eternally alone, dwells with His creatures? Must your betrothed die in a fire, or disappear before your eyes in the green depths of the ocean, for it to be revealed to you for an instant that the last limits of the kingdom of love transcend perhaps the scarcely visible flames of Mira, Altair or Berenice's tresses? Had your eyes been open, might you not have beheld in a kiss that which to-day you perceive in a catastrophe? Are the divine recollections that slumber in our souls to be awakened only by the lance-thrusts of grief? The sage needs no such violent arousing. He sees a tear, a maiden's gesture, a drop of water that falls; he listens to a passing thought, presses a brother's hand, approaches a lip, with open eyes and open soul. He never ceases to behold that of which you have caught but a passing glimpse; and a smile will readily tell him all that it needed a tempest, or even the hand of death, to reveal to you.

For what are in reality the things we call 'Wisdom,' 'Virtue,' 'Heroism,' 'sublime hours,' and 'great moments of life,' but the moments when we have more or less issued forth from ourselves, and have been able to halt, be it only for an instant, on the step of one of the eternal gates whence we see that the faintest cry, the most colourless thought, and most nerveless gestures do not drop into nothingness; or that if they do indeed thus drop, the fall itself is so immense that it suffices to give an august character to our life? Why wait till the firmament shall open amid the roar of the thunderbolt? We must watch for the happy moments when it opens in silence; and it is ever thus opening. You seek God in your life, and you say God appears not. But in what life are there not thousands of hours akin to the hour in that drama where all are waiting for the divine intervention, and none perceive it, till an invisible thought that has flitted across the consciousness of a dying man suddenly reveals itself, and an old man cries out, sobbing for joy and terror, 'But God, there is God!'....

Must we always be warned, and can we only fall on our knees when some one is there to tell us that God is passing by? If you have loved profoundly you have needed no one to tell you that your soul was a thing as great in itself as the world; that the stars, the flowers, the waves of night and sea were not solitary; that it was on the threshold of appearances that everything began, but nothing ended, and that the very lips you kissed belonged to a creature who was loftier, much purer, and much more beautiful than the one whom your arms enfolded. You have beheld that which in life cannot be seen without ecstasy. But cannot we live as though we always loved? It was this that the saints and heroes did; this and nothing more. Ah! truly too much of our life is spent in waiting, like the blind men in the legend who had travelled far so that they might hear their God. They were seated on the steps, and when asked what they were doing in the courtyard of the sanctuary, 'We are waiting,' they replied, shaking their heads, 'and God has not yet said a single word.' But they had not seen that the brass doors of the temple were closed, and they knew not that the edifice was resounding with the voice of their God. Never for an instant does God cease to speak; but no one thinks of opening the doors. And yet, with a little watchfulness, it were not difficult to hear the word that God must speak concerning our every act.

We all live in the sublime. Where else can we live? That is the only place of life. And if aught be lacking, it is not the chance of living in heaven, rather is it watchfulness and meditation, also perhaps a little ecstasy of soul. Though you have but a little room, do you fancy that God is not there, too, and that it is impossible to live therein a life that shall be somewhat lofty? If you complain of being alone, of the absence of events, of loving no one and being unloved, do you think that the words are true? Do you imagine that one can possibly be alone, that love can be a thing one knows, a thing one sees; that events can be weighed like the gold and silver of ransom? Cannot a living thought—proud or humble, it matters not; so it come but from your soul, it is great for you—cannot a lofty desire, or simply a moment of solemn watchfulness to life, enter a little room? And if you love not, or are unloved, and can yet see with some depth of insight that thousands of things are beautiful, that the soul is great and life almost unspeakably earnest, is that not as beautiful as though you loved or were loved? And if the sky itself is hidden from you, 'does not the great starry sky,' asks the poet, 'spread over our soul, in spite of all, under guise of death?' ... All that happens to us is divinely great, and we are always in the centre of a great world. But we must accustom ourselves to live like an angel who has just sprung to life, like a woman who loves, or a man on the point of death. If you knew that you were going to die to-night, or merely that you would have to go away and never return, would you, looking upon men and things for the last time, see them in the same light that you have hitherto seen them? Would you not love as you never yet have loved? Is it the virtue or evil of the appearances around you that would be magnified? Would it be given you to behold the beauty or the ugliness of the soul? Would not everything, down to actual evil and suffering, be transformed into love, overflowing with gentlest tears? Does not, to quote the sage, each opportunity for pardon rob departure or death of something of its bitterness? And yet, in the radiance or sorrow or death, is it towards truth or error that one has taken the last steps one is allowed to take?

Is it the living or the dying who can see and are in the right? Ah! thrice happy they who have thought, spoken, and acted so as to receive the approval of those who are about to die, or to whom a great sorrow has given clearer insight! The sage, to whom none would hearken in life, can meet with no sweeter reward. If you have lived in obscure beauty, you have no cause for disquiet. At the end there must always sound within the heart of man an hour of supreme justice; and misfortune opens eyes that were never open before. Who knows whether at this very moment your shadow be not passing over the soul of a dying man and be not recognised by him as the shadow of one who already knew the truth? May it not be at the bedside of the last agony that is woven the veritable and most precious crown of sage and hero, and of all who have known how to live earnestly amid the sorrows, lofty, pure, and discreet, of life according to the soul?

'Death,' says Lavater, 'does not only beautify our inanimate form; nay, the mere thought of death gives a more beautiful form to life itself.' And even so does every thought, that is infinite as death, beautify our life. But we must not deceive ourselves. To every man there come noble thoughts, that pass across his heart like great white birds. Alas! they do not count; they are strangers whom we are surprised to see, whom we dismiss with importunate gesture. Their time is too short to touch our life. Our soul will not become earnest and deep-searching, as is the soul of the angels, for that we have, for one fleeting instant, beheld the universe in the shadow of death or eternity, in the radiance of joy or the flames of beauty and love. We have all known moments such as these, moments that have but left worthless ashes behind. These things must be habitual with us; it is of no avail that they should come by chance. We must learn to live in a beauty, an earnestness, that shall have become part of ourselves. In life, there is no creature so degraded but knows full well which is the noble and beautiful thing that he should do; but this noble and beautiful thing is not strong enough within him. It is this invisible and abstract strength that it must be our endeavour to increase, first of all. And this strength increases only in those who have acquired the habit of resting, more frequently than others, upon the summits where life absorbs the soul, upon the heights whence we see that every act and every thought are infallibly bound up with something great and immortal. Look upon men and things with the inner eye, with its form and desire, never forgetting that the shadow they throw as they pass by, upon hillock or wall, is but the fleeting image of a mightier shadow, which, like the wing of an imperishable swan, floats over every soul that draws near to their soul. Do not believe that thoughts such as these can be mere ornaments, and without influence upon the lives of those who admit them. It is far more important that one's life should be perceived than that it should be transformed; for no sooner has it been perceived, than it transforms itself of its own accord. These thoughts of which I speak make up the secret treasure of heroism; and, on the day that life compels us to disclose this treasure, we are startled to find therein no forces other than those by which we are impelled towards perfect beauty. Then it is no longer necessary that a great king should die for us to remember that 'the world does not end at the house-doors,' and not an evening passes but the smallest thing suffices to ennoble the soul.

Yet it is not by telling yourself that God is great and that you move in His radiance, that you will be able to live in the beauty and fertile depths where the heroes dwelt. You may perhaps remind yourself, day and night, that the hands of all the invisible powers are waving over your head like a tent with countless folds, and yet shall the least gesture of these hands be imperceptible to you. It behoves you to be keenly vigilant; and better had you watch in the market-place than slumber in the temple. Beauty and grandeur are everywhere; for it needs but an unexpected incident to reveal them to us. This is known to nearly all men; but know it though they may, it is only when fortune or death lashes them that they grope around the wall of life in search of the crevices through which God may be seen. They know full well that there are eternal crevices even in the humble walls of a hovel, and that the smallest window cannot take away a line or a star from the immensity of heavenly space. But it is not enough to possess a truth; it is essential that the truth should possess us.

And yet are we in a world where the smallest events assume, spontaneously, a beauty that ever becomes purer and loftier. There is nothing that coalesces more readily than earth and sky; if your eyes have rested upon the stars, before enfolding in your arms the woman you love, your embrace will not be the same as though you had merely looked at the walls of your room. Be sure that the day you lingered to follow a ray of light through a crevice in the door of life, you did something as great as though you had bandaged the wounds of your enemy, for at that moment did you no longer have any enemies.

Our lives must be spent seeking our God, for God hides; but His artifices, once they be known, seem so simple and smiling! From that moment, the merest nothing reveals His presence, and the greatness of our life depends on so little! Even thus may the verse of a poet, in the midst of the humble incidents of ordinary days, suddenly reveal to us something that is stupendous. No solemn word has been pronounced, and we feel that nothing has been called forth; and yet, why has an ineffable face beckoned to us from behind an old man's tears, why does a vast night, starred with angels, extend over the smile of a child, and why, around a yes or no, murmured by a soul that sings and busies itself with other matters, do we suddenly hold our breath for an instant and say to ourselves, 'Here is the house of God, and this one of the approaches to heaven'?

It is because these poets have been more heedful than we to the 'never-ending shadow.' ... That is the essence of supreme poetry, that, and that alone, and its sole aim is to keep open 'the great road that leads from the seen to the unseen.' But that is life's supreme aim, too, and it is easier far to attain in life than in the noblest of poems, for these have had to abandon the two great wings of silence. Not a single day is trivial. It is essential that this idea should sink into our life and take root therein. There is no question of being sad. Small joys, faint smiles, and great tears, all these fill up the same nook in time and space. You can play in life as innocently 'as a child about a death-bed,' and it is not the tears that are indispensable. Smiles as well as tears open the gates of the other world. Go or come, you will find all you need in the darkness, but never forget that you are close to the gate.

*

After this lengthy digression, I return to my starting-point, which was that 'it is well that men should be reminded that the very humblest of them has the power to fashion, after a divine model that he chooses not, a great moral personality, composed in equal parts of himself and the ideal.' It is only in the depths of life that this 'great moral personality' can be carved out; and only by means of incessant 'revelations of the divine' can we add to the stores of the ideal we require. To every man is it given to attain in spirit to the heights of virtuous life, and to know at all times what his conduct should be, would he act like a hero or a saint. But more than this is needed. It is essential that the spiritual atmosphere about us should be transformed to such a degree that it ends by resembling the atmosphere of Swedenborg's beautiful countries of the age of gold, wherein the air permitted not a falsehood to leave the lips. An instant comes then, when the smallest ill that we fain would commit falls at our feet like a leaden ball upon a disc of bronze; when everything changes, though we know it not, into beauty, love, or truth. But this atmosphere enwraps those only who have been heedful to ventilate their life sufficiently by at times flinging open the gates of the other world. It is when we are near to those gates that we see; it is when we are near to those gates that we love. For to love one's neighbour does not mean only to give oneself to him, to serve, help, and sustain others. We may possibly be neither good, nor noble, nor beautiful, even in the midst of the greatest sacrifice; and the sister of charity who dies by the bedside of a typhoid patient may perchance have a mean, rancorous, miserable soul. To love one's neighbour in the immovable depths means to love in others that which is eternal; for one's neighbour, in the truest sense of the term, is that which approaches the nearest to God; in other words, all that is best and purest in man; and it is only by ever lingering near the gates I spoke of, that you can discover the divine in the soul. Then will you be able to say with the great Jean Paul: 'When I desire to love most tenderly one who is dear to me, and wish to forgive him everything, I have but to look at him for a few moments in silence.' To learn to love, one must first learn to see. 'I lived for twenty years by my sister's side,' said a friend to me, one day, 'and *I saw her* for the first time at the moment of our mother's death.' Here, too, it had been necessary that death should violently fling open an eternal gate, so that two souls might behold each other in a ray of the primeval light. Is there one amongst us who has not near to him sisters he has never seen?

Happily, even in those whose vision is most limited, there is always something that acts in silence as though they had seen. It is possible, perhaps, that to be good is only to be in a little light what all are in darkness. Therefore, doubtless, is it well that we should endeavour to raise our life, and should strive towards summits where ill-doing becomes impossible. And therefore, too, is it well to accustom the eye to behold events and men in a divine atmosphere. But even that is not indispensable; and how small must the difference seem to the eyes of a God! We are in a world where truth reigns at the bottom of things, and where it is not truth but falsehood that needs to be explained. If the happiness of your brother sadden you, do not despise yourself; you will not have to travel far along the road before you will come across something in yourself that will not be saddened. And even though you do not travel the road, it matters little: something there was that was not sad....

Those who think of nothing have the same truth as those who think of God; the truth is a little further from the threshold, that is all. 'Even in the life that is most ordinary,' says Renan, 'the part that is done for God is enormous. The lowest of men would rather be just than unjust: we all worship, we all pray, numbers of times every day, without knowing it.' And we are surprised when chance suddenly reveals to us the importance of this divine part. There are about us thousands and thousands of poor creatures who have nothing of beauty in their lives: they come, they go, in obscurity, and we believe that all is dead within them; and no one pays any heed. And then one day a simple word, an unexpected silence, a little tear that springs from the source of beauty itself, tell us that they have found the means of raising aloft, in the shadow of their soul, an ideal a thousand times more beautiful than the most beautiful things their ears have ever heard, or their eyes ever seen. Oh, noble and pallid ideals of silence and shadow! It is you, above all, who call forth the smile of the angels, it is you, above all, who soar direct to God! In what myriads of hovels, in what dens of misery, in what prisons, perhaps, are you not being cherished at this moment, cherished with the purest blood and tears of an unhappy soul that has never smiled; even as the bees, at the time when all the flowers are dead about them, still offer to her who is to be their queen a honey a thousand times more precious than the honey they give to their little sisters of daily life.... Which of us has not met, more than once, along the paths of life, a forsaken soul that has yet not lost the courage to cherish, in the darkness, a thought diviner and purer than all those that so many others had the power to choose in the light? Here, too, it is simplicity that is God's favourite slave; and it is enough, perhaps, that a few sages should know what has to be done, for the rest of us to act as though we knew too....

THE INNER BEAUTY

NOTHING in the whole world is so athirst for beauty as the soul, nor is there anything to which beauty clings so readily. There is nothing in the world capable of such spontaneous up-lifting, of such speedy ennoblement; nothing that offers more scrupulous obedience to the pure and noble commands it receives. There is nothing in the world that yields deeper submission to the empire of a thought that is loftier than other thoughts. And on this earth of ours there are but few souls that can withstand the dominion of the soul that has suffered itself to become beautiful.

In all truth might it be said that beauty is the unique aliment of our soul, for in all places does it search for beauty, and it perishes not of hunger even in the most degraded of lives. For indeed nothing of beauty can pass by and be altogether unperceived. Perhaps does it never pass by save only in our unconsciousness, but its action is no less puissant in gloom of night than by light of day; the joy it procures may be less tangible, but other difference there is none. Look at the most ordinary of men, at a time when a little beauty has contrived to steal into their darkness. They have come together, it matters not where, and for no special reason; but no sooner are they assembled than their very first thought would seem to be to close the great doors of life. Yet has each one of them, when alone, more than once lived in accord with his soul. He has loved perhaps, of a surety he has suffered. Inevitably must he, too, have heard the 'sounds that come from the distant country of Splendour and Terror'; and many an evening has he bowed down in silence before laws that are deeper than the sea. And yet when these men are assembled it is with the basest of things that they love to debauch themselves. They have a strange indescribable fear of beauty, and as their number increases so does this fear become greater, resembling indeed their dread of silence or of a verity that is too pure. And so true is this that, were one of them to have done something heroic in the course of the day, he would ascribe wretched motives to his conduct, thereby endeavouring to find excuses for it, and these motives would lie readily to his hand in that lower region where he and his fellows were assembled. And yet listen: a proud and lofty word has been spoken, a word that has in a measure undammed the springs of life. For one instant has a soul dared to reveal itself, even such as it is in love and sorrow, such as it is in face of death and in the solitude that dwells around the stars of night. Disquiet prevails, on some faces there is astonishment, others smile. But have you never felt at moments such as those how unanimous is the fervour wherewith every soul admires, and how unspeakably even the very feeblest, from the remotest depths of its dungeon, approves the word it has recognised as akin to itself? For they have all suddenly sprung to life again in the primitive and normal atmosphere that is their own; and could you but hearken with angels' ears, I doubt not but you would hear mightiest applause in that kingdom of amazing radiance wherein the souls do dwell. Do you not think that even the most timid of them would take courage unto themselves were but similar words to be spoken every evening? Do you not think that men would live purer lives? And yet though the word come not again, still will something momentous have happened, that must leave still more momentous trace behind. Every evening will its sisters recognise the soul that pronounced the word, and henceforth, be the conversation never so trivial, its mere presence will, I know not how, add thereto something of majesty. Whatever else betide, there has been a change that we cannot determine. No longer will such absolute power be vested in the baser side of things, and henceforth, even the most terror stricken of souls will know that there is somewhere a place of refuge....

Certain it is that the natural and primitive relationship of soul to soul is a relationship of beauty. For beauty is the only language of our soul; none other is known to it. It has no other life, it can produce nothing else, in nothing else can it take interest. And therefore it is that the most oppressed, nay, the most degraded of souls—if it may truly be said that a soul can be degraded—immediately hail with acclamation every thought, every word or deed, that is great and beautiful. Beauty is the only element wherewith the soul is organically connected, and it has no other standard of judgment. This is brought home to us at every moment of our life, and is no less evident to the man by whom beauty may more than once have been denied than to him who is ever seeking it in his heart. Should a day come when you stand in profoundest need of another's sympathy, would you go to him who was wont to greet the passage of beauty with a sneering smile? Would you go to him whose shake of the head had sullied a generous action or a mere impulse that was pure? Even though perhaps you had been of those who commended him, you would none the less, when it was truth that knocked at your door, turn to the man who had known how to prostrate himself and love. In its very depths had your soul passed its judgment, and it is this silent and unerring judgment that will rise to the surface, after thirty years perhaps, and send you towards a sister who shall be more truly you than you are yourself, for that she has been nearer to beauty....

There needs but so little to encourage beauty in our soul; so little to awaken the slumbering angels; or perhaps is there no need of awakening—it is enough that we lull them not to sleep. It requires more effort to fall, perhaps, than to rise. Can we, without putting constraint upon ourselves, confine our thoughts to everyday things at times when the sea stretches before us, and we are face to face with the night? And what soul is there but knows that it is ever confronting the sea, ever in presence of an eternal night? Did we but dread beauty less it would come about that nought else in life would be visible; for in reality it is beauty that underlies everything, it is beauty alone that exists. There is no soul but is conscious of this, none that is not in readiness; but where are those that hide not their beauty? And yet must one of them 'begin.' Why not dare to be the one to 'begin'? The others are all watching eagerly around us like little children in front of a marvellous palace. They press upon the threshold, whispering to each other and peering through every crevice, but there is not one who dares put his shoulder to the door. They are all waiting for some grown-up person to come and fling it open. But hardly ever does such a one pass by.

And yet what is needed to become the grown-up person for whom they lie in wait? So little! The soul is not exacting. A thought that is almost beautiful—a thought that you speak not, but that you cherish within you at this moment, will irradiate you as though you were a transparent vase. They will see it and their greeting to you will be very different than had you been meditating how best to deceive your brother. We are surprised when certain men tell us that they have never come across real ugliness, that they cannot conceive that a soul can be base. Yet need there be no cause for surprise. These men had 'begun.' They themselves had been the first to be beautiful, and had therefore attracted all the beauty that passed by, as a lighthouse attracts the vessels from the four corners of the horizon. Some there are who complain of women, for instance, never dreaming that, the first time a man meets a woman, a single word or thought that denies the beautiful or profound will be enough to poison for ever *his existence* in her soul. 'For my part,' said a sage to me one day, 'I have never come across a single woman who did not bring to me something that was great.' He was great himself first of all; therein lay his secret. There is one thing only that the soul can never forgive; it is to have been compelled to behold, or share, or pass close to an ugly action, word, or thought. It cannot forgive, for forgiveness here were but the denial of itself. And yet with the generality of men, ingenuity, strength and skill do but imply that the soul must first of all be banished from their life, and that every impulse that lies too deep must be carefully brushed aside. Even in love do they act thus, and therefore it is that the woman, who is so much nearer the truth, can scarcely ever live a moment of the true life with them. It is as though men dreaded the contact of their soul, and were anxious to keep its beauty at immeasurable distance. Whereas, on the contrary, we should endeavour to move in advance of ourselves. If at this moment you think or say something that is too beautiful to be true in you—if you have but endeavoured to think or say it to-day, on the morrow it will be true. We must try to be more beautiful than ourselves; we shall never distance our soul. We can never err when it is question of silent or hidden beauty. Besides, so long as the spring within us be limpid, it matters but little whether error there be or not. But do any of us ever dream of making the slightest unseen effort? And yet in the domain where we are everything is effective, for that everything is waiting. All the doors are unlocked, we have but to push them open, and the palace is full of manacled queens. A single word will very often suffice to clear the mountain of refuse. Why not have the courage to meet a base question with a noble answer? Do you imagine it would pass quite unnoticed or merely arouse surprise? Do you not think it would be more akin to the discourse that would naturally be held between two souls? We know not where it may give encouragement, where freedom. Even he who rejects your words will, in spite of himself, have taken a step towards the beauty that is within him. Nothing of beauty dies without having purified something, nor can aught of beauty be lost. Let us not be afraid of sowing it along the road. It may remain there for weeks or years, but like the diamond it cannot dissolve, and finally there will pass by some one whom its glitter will attract; he will pick it up and go his way, rejoicing. Then why keep back a lofty, beautiful word, for that you doubt whether others will understand? An instant of higher goodness was impending over you; why hinder its coming, even though you believe not that those about you will profit thereby? What if you are among men of the valley, is that sufficient reason for checking the instinctive movement of your soul towards the mountain peaks? Does darkness rob deep feeling of its power? Have the blind nought but their eyes wherewith to distinguish those who love them from those who love them not? Can the beauty not exist that is not understood, and is there not in every man something that does understand—in regions far beyond what he seems to understand, far beyond, too, what he believes he understands? 'Even to the very wretchedest of all,' said to me one day the loftiest minded creature it has ever been my happiness to know, 'even to the very wretchedest of all I never have the courage to say anything in reply that is ugly or mediocre.' I have for a long time followed that man's life, and have seen the inexplicable power he exercised over the most obscure, the most unapproachable, the blindest, even the most rebellious of souls. For no tongue can tell the power of a soul that strives to live in an atmosphere of beauty, and is actively beautiful in itself. And indeed is it not the quality of this activity that renders a life either miserable or divine?

If we could but probe to the root of things it might well be discovered that it is by the strength of some souls that are beautiful that others are sustained in life. Is it not the idea we each form of certain chosen ones that constitutes the only living, effective morality? But in this idea how much is there of the soul that is chosen, how much of him who chooses? Do not these things blend very mysteriously, and does not this ideal morality lie infinitely deeper than the morality of the most beautiful books? A far-reaching influence exists therein whose limits it is indeed difficult to define, and a fountain of strength whereat we all of us drink many times a day. Would not any weakness in one of those creatures whom you thought perfect and loved in the region of beauty, at once lessen your confidence in the universal greatness of things, and would your admiration for them suffer?

And again, I doubt whether anything in the world can beautify a soul more spontaneously, more naturally, than the knowledge that somewhere in its neighbourhood there exists a pure and noble being whom it can unreservedly love. When the soul has veritably drawn near to such a being, beauty is no longer a lovely, lifeless thing that one exhibits to the stranger, for it suddenly takes unto itself an imperious existence, and its activity becomes so natural as to be henceforth irresistible. Wherefore you will do well to think it over, for none are alone, and those who are good must watch.

Plotinus, in the eighth book of the fifth 'Ennead,' after speaking of the beauty that is 'intelligible'—*i.e.*, divine, concludes thus: 'As regards ourselves, we are beautiful when we belong to ourselves, and ugly when we lower ourselves to our inferior nature. Also are we beautiful when we know ourselves, and ugly when we have no such knowledge.' Bear it in mind, however, that here we are on the mountains, where not to know oneself means far more than mere ignorance of what takes place within us at moments of jealousy or love, fear or envy, happiness or unhappiness. Here not to know oneself means to be unconscious of all the divine that throbs in man. As we wander from the gods within us so does ugliness enwrap us; as we discover them, so do we become more beautiful. But it is only by revealing the divine that is in us that we may discover the divine in others. Needs must one god beckon to another, and no signal is so imperceptible but they will every one of them respond. It cannot be said too often that, be the crevice never so small, it will yet suffice for all the waters of heaven to pour into our soul. Every cup is stretched out to the unknown spring, and we are in a region where none think of aught but beauty. If we could ask of an angel what it is that our souls do in the shadow, I believe the angel would answer, after having looked for many years perhaps, and seen far more than the things the soul seems to do in the eyes of men, 'They transform into beauty all the little things that are given to them.' Ah! we must admit that the human soul is possessed of singular courage! Resignedly does it labour, its whole life long, in the darkness whither most of us relegate it, where it is spoken to by none. There, never complaining, does it do all that in its power lies, striving to tear from out the pebbles we fling to it the nucleus of eternal light that peradventure they contain. And in the midst of its work it is ever lying in wait for the moment when it may show, to a sister who is more tenderly cared for, or who chances to be nearer, the treasures it has so toilfully amassed. But thousands of existences there are that no sister visits; thousands of existences wherein life has infused such timidity into the soul that it departs without saying a word, without even once having been able to deck itself with the humblest jewels of its humble crown....

And yet, in spite of all, does it watch over everything from out its invisible heaven. It warns and loves, it admires, attracts, repels. At every fresh event does it rise to the surface, where it lingers till it be thrust down again, being looked upon as wearisome and insane. It wanders to and fro, like Cassandra at the gates of the Atrides. It is ever giving utterance to words of shadowy truth, but there are none to listen. When we raise our eyes it yearns for a ray of sun or star, that it may weave into a thought, or, haply, an impulse, which shall be unconscious and very pure. And if our eyes bring it nothing, still will it know how to turn its pitiful disillusion into something ineffable, that it will conceal even till its death. When we love, how eagerly does it drink in the light from behind the closed door—keen with expectation, it yet wastes not a minute, and the light that steals through the apertures becomes beauty and truth to the soul. But if the door opens not (and how many lives are there wherein it does open?) it will go back into its prison, and its regret will perhaps be a loftier verity that shall never be seen, for we are now in the region of transformations whereof none may speak; and though nothing born this side of the door can be lost, yet does it never mingle with our life....

I said just now that the soul changed into beauty the little things we gave to it. It would even seem, the more we think of it, that the soul has no other reason for existence, and that all its activity is consumed in amassing, at the depths of us, a treasure of indescribable beauty. Might not everything naturally turn into beauty, were we not unceasingly interrupting the arduous labours of our soul? Does not evil itself become precious so soon as it has gathered therefrom the deep lying diamond of repentance? The acts of injustice whereof you have been guilty, the tears you have caused to flow, will not these end too by becoming so much radiance and love in your soul? Have you ever cast your eyes into this kingdom of purifying flame that is within you? Perhaps a great wrong may have been done you to-day, the act itself being mean and disheartening, the mode of action of the basest, and ugliness wrapped you round as your tears fell. But let some years elapse, then give one look into your soul, and tell me whether, beneath the recollection of that act, you see not something that is already purer than thought; an indescribable, unnameable force that has nought in common with the forces of this world; a mysterious inexhaustible spring of the other life, whereat you may drink for the rest of your days. And yet will you have rendered no assistance to the untiring queen; other thoughts will have filled your mind, and it will be without your knowledge that the act will have been purified in the silence of your being, and will have flown into the precious waters that lie in the great reservoir of truth and beauty, which, unlike the shallower reservoir of true or beautiful thoughts, has an ever unruffled surface, and remains for all time out of reach of the breath of life. Emerson tells us that there is not an act or event in our life but, sooner or later, casts off its outer shell, and bewilders us by its sudden flight, from the very depths of us, on high into the empyrean. And this is true to a far greater extent than Emerson had foreseen, for the further we advance in these regions, the diviner are the spheres we discover.

We can form no adequate conception of what this silent activity of the souls that surround us may really mean. Perhaps you have spoken a pure word to one of your fellows by whom it has not been understood. You look upon it as lost and dismiss it from your mind. But one day, peradventure, the word comes up again extraordinarily transformed, and revealing the unexpected fruit it has borne in the darkness; then silence once more falls over all. But it matters not; we have learned that nothing can be lost in the soul, and that even to the very pettiest there come moments of splendour. It is unmistakably borne home to us that even the unhappiest and the most destitute of men have at the depths of their being and in spite of themselves a treasure of beauty that they cannot despoil. They have but to acquire the habit of dipping into this treasure. It suffices not that beauty should keep solitary festival in life; it has to become a festival of every day. There needs no great effort to be admitted into the ranks of those 'whose eyes no longer behold earth in flower and sky in glory in infinitesimal fragments, but indeed in sublime masses,' and I speak here of flowers and sky that are purer and more lasting than those that we behold. Thousands of channels there are through which the beauty of our soul may sail even unto our thoughts. Above all is there the wonderful, central channel of love.

Is it not in love that are found the purest elements of beauty that we can offer to the soul? Some there are who do thus in beauty love each other. And to love thus means that, little by little, the sense of ugliness is lost; that one's eyes are closed to all the littlenesses of life, to all but the freshness and virginity of the very humblest of souls. Loving thus, we have no longer even the need to forgive. Loving thus, we can no longer have anything to conceal, for that the ever-present soul transforms all things into beauty. It is to behold evil in so far only as it purifies indulgence, and teaches us no longer to confound the sinner with his sin. Loving thus do we raise on high within ourselves all those about us who have attained an eminence where failure has become impossible; heights whence a paltry action has so far to fall that, touching earth, it is compelled to yield up its diamond soul. It is to transform, though all unconsciously, the feeblest intention that hovers about us into illimitable movement. It is to summon all that is beautiful in earth, heaven or soul, to the banquet of love. Loving thus, we do indeed exist before our fellows as we exist before God. It means that the least gesture will call forth the presence of the soul with all its treasure. No longer is there need of death, disaster or tears for that the soul shall appear; a smile suffices. Loving thus, we perceive truth in happiness as profoundly as some of the heroes perceived it in the radiance of greatest sorrow. It means that the beauty that turns into love is undistinguishable from the love that turns into beauty. It means to be able no longer to tell where the ray of a star leaves off and the kiss of an ordinary thought begins. It means to have come so near to God that the angels possess us. Loving thus, the same soul will have been so beautified by us all that it will become, little by little, the 'unique angel' mentioned by Swedenborg. It means that each day will reveal to us a new beauty in that mysterious angel, and that we shall walk together in a goodness that shall ever become more and more living, loftier and loftier. For there exists also a lifeless beauty, made up of the past alone; but the veritable love renders the past useless, and its approach creates a boundless future of goodness, without disaster and without tears. To love thus is but to free one's soul, and to become as beautiful as the soul thus freed. 'If, in the emotion that this spectacle cannot fail to awaken in thee,' says the great Plotinus, when dealing with kindred matters—and of all the intellects known to me that of Plotinus draws the nearest to the divine—'If, in the emotion that this spectacle cannot fail to awaken in thee, thou proclaimest not that it is beautiful; and if, plunging thine eyes into thyself, thou dost not then feel the charm of beauty, it is in vain that, thy disposition being such, thou shouldst seek the intelligible beauty; for thou wouldst seek it only with that which is ugly and impure. Therefore it is that the discourse we hold here is not addressed to all men. But if thou hast recognised beauty within thyself, see that thou rise to the recollection of the intelligible beauty.'

Milton Keynes UK
Ingram Content Group UK Ltd.
UKHW030704170824
447045UK00004B/418